Deciphering
THE LOST SYMBOL

D0981435

Deciphering
THE LOST SYMBOL

Freemasons, Myths and the Mysteries of Washington, D.C.

Christopher L. Hodapp

Ulysses Press

Published by: ULYSSES PRESS
　　　　　　　P.O. Box 3440
　　　　　　　Berkeley, CA 94703
　　　　　　　www.ulyssespress.com

Portions of this book have appeared previously in *Solomon's Builders: Freemasons, Founding Fathers and the Secrets of Washington, D.C.*

ISBN-13: 978-1-56975-773-4
Library of Congress Control Number: 2009940328

Printed in Canada by Webcom

10 9 8 7 6 5 4 3 2 1

Acquisitions Editor: Kelly Reed
Managing Editor: Claire Chun
Editor: Teresa Castle
Proofreader: Lauren Harrison
Index: Sayre Van Young

Distributed by Publishers Group West

To the Brethren.

✦ ✦ ✦

Table of Contents

>JULO CC LCO>OO>V

Acknowledgments

If ever there was a month to be a Mason in the Washington area, it was September of 2009.

My deepest thanks go to Rex Hucthens and especially to Art de Hoyos and S. Brent Morris at the House of the Temple for their friendship and their knowledge of all things Scottish Rite, and to my friend Mark Tabbert at the George Washington Masonic Memorial.

My gratitude goes to the members of the Masonic Society for their patience as I concentrated on this book instead of getting their Journal to them in a timely manner, and to Randy Williams and Jay Hochberg for covering for me. And, of course, to my friends Nathan Brindle, Jim Dillman, and Roger VanGorden for their ongoing support.

Hats off to the whole Ulysses Press team who made this book happen in record time: Nick Denton-Brown, who invited me to their party to begin with; Bryce Willett, who believed in this book before anyone else; Kelly Reed, for getting it started; Claire Chun, for her endless patience; and especially Teresa Castle, for understanding that a run-on sentence is just my style.

To my wife, researcher, historian, writing partner, and organizer of my life, Alice, who kept sanity in the house. Nothing I do would be possible without her.

And finally, to Dan Brown, who has reminded the world about who and what the Freemasons are, what they believe in, and why they remain important to society.

Introduction

⌐□>⌐⊡⊐<L>⌐⊡□

There is a key to every Mystery, and every such key has
been so effectively hidden that centuries have elapsed,
in some cases, before its discovery…

I. EDWARD CLARK, *THE ROYAL SECRET*

In May 2004, the reclusive author Dan Brown made a rare speech in
Concord, New Hampshire, and revealed that his sequel to *The Da
Vinci Code* would be about the Freemasons. He added that Masons
should welcome this news because there is so much misinformation
about the group.[1] Was he ever right. After teasing the world for six
years, in the summer of 2009, Brown finally delivered his much-
anticipated sequel. Brown's *The Lost Symbol* is a 509-page love letter
to the fraternity of Freemasonry.

Like Brown's previous novels, *Angels & Demons* and *The Da
Vinci Code*, the book again features the fictional, tweed-jacketed, mys-
tery-solving Harvard professor and "symbologist" Robert Langdon
running at breakneck speed through a familiar landscape—Washington, D.C.—filled with unfamiliar places, people, philosophy, history, art, science, and religion.

When *The Da Vinci Code* was first published in 2003, Dan
Brown had intentionally placed clues within the cover's artwork about
his next novel's subject. As Brown's readers know, his books make fre-
quent use of puzzles, symbolism, and secret-code breaking, and on
the inside paper flaps of the original hardback edition, certain letters
were printed darker than others. When copied down in order, they
revealed a phrase that is of ritualistic significance to the fraternity of
Freemasons: *Is there no help for the widow's son?* This is part of a tradi-

tional signal of Masonic distress. (It was also a signal that Brown probably wasn't going to be writing about the League of Women Voters.) The first announced title of the book was *The Solomon Key*, evoking the biblical story of the building of King Solomon's Temple in 1000 B.C., which is central to Freemasonry's ritual ceremonies and mythical origins. Masons were excited, but nervous as well. After all, they might wind up being portrayed as Opus Dei had been in *The Da Vinci Code*, as a bizarre, mysterious organization that harbors evil, bald-headed, albino assassins, or plots nefarious murders of popes, cardinals, and Interpol agents.

In the run-up to *The Lost Symbol's* release, Masons became even more nervous. In keeping with Brown's past novels, there was symbolism to be found not just in the narrative, but outside of it. Even the release date of 9/15/09 was significant: the numbers add up to 33, a number central to the Masonic hierarchy. The U.S. version of the cover depicted a wax seal featuring a double-headed eagle, the number 33, and the Latin phrase, *Ordo ab Chao*, or Order from Chaos, the motto of the Scottish Rite of Freemasonry; the seal was set against a background of symbols of the zodiac and alchemy, which was another cause for concern.

Meanwhile, across the Atlantic, the United Kingdom's version of the cover displayed a flaming key with a Masonic square and compasses. That symbol is similar to a graphic device used by Freemason and author Robert Lomas in a series of books that use the term "The Hiram Key," and it was clearly meant to echo the originally planned title of the book, *The Solomon Key*.

Once *The Lost Symbol* was published, tense speculation ended at last. Freemasonry does indeed appear throughout the book, and it is central to the story. The very real Washington, D.C., headquarters of the Scottish Rite Southern Jurisdiction, the House of the Temple, is the setting for important, and harrowing, sequences in the thriller. However, to the relief of Masons, the book did not present them as treacherous supervillains; instead, it was almost reverential in its treatment of the fraternity.

If you haven't read it yet, here's the non-spoiler description of the plot. Robert Langdon is called to Washington to give a speech at the U.S. Capitol, but it turns out to be a clever ruse by a bald, tattoo-covered evil genius named Mal'akh who is in search of the deepest secrets to Life, the Universe, and Everything—secrets that supposedly are held by the Freemasons. The story involves a pint-sized stone pyramid encoded with symbols that eventually point the way to the secret knowledge of "Ancient Mysteries" passed down through the centuries and protected by the Masons. Langdon has to save his mentor, Peter Solomon, and Solomon's sister, Katherine, from the bad guy and keep this evil genius from exposing a Masonic secret that could bring down the whole U.S. government if it were to be made public. Along the way, you get Brown's brand of bewildering, nonstop *didja knows?* and historical tidbits, along with his trademark two-page chapters, so you blast through it like a jumbo box of popcorn.

That ends the non-spoiler portion of this book. If you haven't read *The Lost Symbol* yet, go do it now, because I won't be squeamish from here on about dishing up the story's twists and turns in order to discuss details in Brown's book and show how they relate to the true history of Freemasonry.

I am a Freemason. Let's just get that out of the way right up front. If you never heard of the Freemasons before you read Dan Brown's *The Lost Symbol*, or if you had vaguely heard of them but were clueless about who or what the Masons are, you've still no doubt noticed that suddenly you're finding them everywhere. As a Mason, I am able to provide an insider's view of what Brown has written because I have experienced Masonic degree ceremonies and been inside the buildings that play an important role in his story. I've studied these Masonic landmarks in depth, and all of them are discussed at length in my previous book, *Solomon's Builders: Freemasons, Founding Fathers and the Secrets of Washington, D.C.*

Dan Brown has stated in his novels that the secret societies and organizations that appear in his novels are based on fact. While groups like the eighteenth-century Bavarian Illuminati and the modern Catholic organization Opus Dei have indeed existed, they usually bear little resemblance to Brown's fictional portrayals. That's the prerogative of the novelist. Unfortunately, readers aren't always aware of the difference between fact and fiction. Even though Dan Brown's treatment of Freemasonry is overwhelmingly positive in *The Lost Symbol*, he does employ some dramatic license concerning the Masons for the sake of his plot.

Few authors would enjoy the truly terrifying assignment of writing the sequel to the sixth most popular book in the history of the English language, especially after giving the world clues about it six years in advance. I am convinced that every time a *National Treasure* movie came out, Brown's wife had to spend three days talking him in off the window ledge. Hoards of second-guessers had time to dream up plot twists about Freemasons and Washington landmarks and then plaster them all over bookstores, movie screens, and the Internet while Brown held his manuscript back. Of course, he was a little busy, what with two lawsuits accusing him of plagiarizing the plot of *The Da Vinci Code*, as well as two big-budget Hollywood films of his books coming out. All the while, that symbolic release date drew nearer. Mystically speaking, this had to go down just so. But the fact is that many fans were a bit annoyed. After all, Nora Roberts or Stephen King could have churned out one or two dozen books in that time.

According to Dan Brown, in a rare interview he granted to NBC's *Dateline*, there was one unexpected reason for the long delay: he was having a blast doing the research. Brown is an academic from a family of academics, and he freely admitted that he had made so much money with *The Da Vinci Code* that he was able to indulge every academic's dream—pure research for the sake of research, particularly on the subject of "noetic science," a funky and fascinating new discipline that few people had ever heard of.

Throughout the summer of 2009, after *The Lost Symbol*'s new title and release date had been announced, the publisher made use of online social networks to promote the book. Using Twitter and Facebook, they toyed with Brown fans who were looking for clues to story points as a series of ciphers, puzzles, anagrams, and logogriphs were gradually released and eagerly solved. Entire blogs were devoted to dissecting these clues, and eager Browniacs were sent off in search of everything from the works of Francis Bacon to Hermes Trismegistus. Eschewing *CSI* reruns, devotees were puzzling over cryptograms, mapping out alleged experimental Air Force aircraft sightings, scrutinizing obscure artwork, and interpreting shadowy manuscripts on alchemy. Unfortunately, after the book's release, it turned out that most of the clues had been written by an advertising agency that had no knowledge whatsoever of what was actually in the book.

Deciphering The Lost Symbol was written to explain and explore the enigmas that really are in the book. It explains where Brown went wrong and where he got it right, not just on the subject of Freemasons but on other aspects of his hero's twelve-hour dash through the nation's capital. It also explores some of the concepts that Brown touched on but left tantalizingly unexplained, as well as some avenues he failed to mention that many fans and armchair quarterbacks had expected.

Because Freemasonry plays a large part in the novel, the fraternity and its symbols, rituals, philosophy, and practices, as well as its role in the founding of the United States and the building of Washington, D.C., will be a big part of the focus of this book. But along the way, I discuss many other elements of *The Lost Symbol*. Brown's practice of piling an almost encyclopedic stack of historic, religious, and cultural asides into his stories provides a wealth of topics to investigate.

Some of what is talked about in this book may sound familiar if you have read my previous book, *Solomon's Builders*. It was written two years before *The Lost Symbol* was published, and some of the concepts and locations in that book necessarily cross paths with this one. I simply ask that you not get impatient when you hit the occasional familiar passage, because these are two very different works, with very different approaches.

✦ ✦ ✦

I was standing on the steps of the House of the Temple at 1733 16th Street NW in Washington shortly after *The Lost Symbol* was released. This monumental building is the headquarters of the Scottish Rite Southern Jurisdiction, which I explain in Chapter 5, and it is the setting of the exciting climax of Brown's book. It is a real building, and it is described in great detail in the novel.

It just so happened that the Scottish Rite Supreme Council was meeting on that day. This was their annual gathering to confer the honor of the 33° (pronounced *thirty-third degree*) upon various candidates, as well as to enjoy banquets and guest speakers and perform the usual sort of annual-meeting administrivia that most companies and organizations indulge in. Brown's book had been released about three weeks before, and I was being interviewed about modern Freemasonry by an overseas TV crew. As we stood there, the reporter got to see two very different sides of the way Masonry is treated in this country in the space of just three minutes.

First, several Masonic brothers from all over the world streamed out of the door, and we all greeted each other warmly. Meanwhile, Masons visiting from out of town wandered up to take pictures and tour the building. One came over to comment about how my book, *Freemasons For Dummies*, had influenced him to join the fraternity and what a profound effect Masonry had had on his life.

Suddenly, a car sped by on 16th Street, horn blaring, as the driver screamed out the window, "*Freaks! Racists! Masons should die!*" Just to make sure we all got the message, he went around the block and did it again.

Not everyone in the world is as admiring of the Freemasons as Dan Brown, and his book has ticked off some people who believe he has unfairly lavished praise on the fraternity. The day *The Lost Symbol* appeared on bookstands, the Catholic League's Bill Donohue angrily wrote, "Dan Brown may loathe Catholics, but he just adores the Masons."[2] Two days later, the BBC asked in a news story, "Can we trust Dan Brown on the Freemasons?"[3] And in a particularly notable screed, the *New York Times's* perennially grouchy columnist Maureen Dowd went off into a full-tilt attack on the book.[4] Describing Brown's novel as a "desperate attempt to ingratiate himself with the Masons," she followed by mocking the fraternity as "the ultimate elite private boys' club" that has "conspired to shape the nation's capital and Western civilization." No doubt they also trip little old ladies, drown puppies, and cheat on their income tax.

And this is just the mild, Ivy League stuff. I haven't even mentioned the outrageous contentions about Freemasonry of Jim Marrs, David Icke, Alex Jones, and a whole horde of commentators who hope to make a fast buck by denouncing the supposedly nefarious activities of the world's most maligned brotherhood. Doubtless in the coming months they, too, will have their say on Dan Brown's positive portrayal of the Masons. So, this book also discusses some of the reasons why Freemasonry has attracted not just your everyday critics but some of the world's most vehement conspiracy theorists and detractors.

✦ ✦ ✦

There are far too many television "documentaries" these days that make wild assertions about history—and in particular about little-known groups like the Freemasons, the Knights Templar, the Rosicrucians, and others—that have absolutely no basis in fact. Sadly, media outlets like The History Channel (now simply known as History™) cannot be trusted to carefully indicate when they are presenting documented facts by well-regarded researchers and when they are purveying preposterous nonsense by wishful thinkers or the perennially delusional. I can't help but think that these same producers would not have the insensitivity to craft a program about Nazi death camps that intercuts Auschwitz survivors with Holocaust deniers, just for the sake of "balance."

Apparently, it seems perfectly reasonable to them to intercut statements by serious Masonic historians with claims by those who believe the Washington Monument, built by the Freemasons, is an alien landing coordinate lying in wait for the day when shape-shifting reptilian creatures from another galaxy descend to meet with their Masonic tools here on Earth to take over the planet and make slaves, or dinner, of us all! Likewise, speculative books are not always labeled as such, and in an age of instantaneous communication, the appearance of a crackpot theory in print is often given the same trappings of credibility as a serious scholarly work. Thus, it is all too easy for a superficial examination of a topic to send the unwary reader tumbling headfirst down a bunny hole of conjecture.

This is something I know a little about. While researching my 2007 book, *Solomon's Builders*, I read Bob Arnebeck's *Through A Fiery Trial*, a mind-numbingly detailed account of the building of America's new Federal City. In the stories of the tumultuous year of 1793, I came across a reference that leapt off the page, screaming "Dan Brown Alert."

In colonial days, the first solid ground on the marshy north shore of the Potomac, just north of where the Lincoln Memorial stands today, was an outcropping of rocks jutting into the river. On several old maps it is cryptically labeled the "Key of All Keys." Its more popular name was Braddock's Rock, reportedly because British General Edward Braddock and his red-coated soldiers, accompanied by young British Lieutenant Colonel George Washington, landed there in 1755. Washington had become a Freemason less than two years before.

During colonial times, the hillside above Braddock's Rock was known as Observatory Hill because it was a great place from which to spot enemy naval vessels moving up the Potomac. British naval ships frequently docked there to drop off troops and supplies. Eventually, in 1844, the Old Naval Observatory was built on top of it. Now, if you are a fan of David Ovason's book *The Secret Architecture of Our Nation's Capital* (I'm not, just for the record), then this observatory business does have a Masonic connection, since Ovason contends that the Masonic designers of Washington were all obsessed with the zodiac.

About 1832, when the old C&O canal was extended below Georgetown to connect with the Washington City Canal, nearly all that was left of the original Braddock's Rock was blasted away. All the riverside swamps were filled in to suppress mosquitoes and the constant malarial fevers that plagued the district. These days, all that remains of the rock is at the bottom of a well near the Kennedy Center, beside the access ramp from Constitution Avenue to the Theodore Roosevelt Bridge on the way to Virginia. Hundreds of commuters drive past the round stone entrance every day without ever giving it a second glance.

But not me. I was sure it was a whole lot more than an abandoned well. I just knew that the "Key of All Keys" was some kind of esoteric reference. It had astronomical connections. It had Masonic connections. It was in the nation's capital. Most important, it had what was undoubtedly an occult name that just had to mean something big.

The stone entrance to Washington, D.C.'s "Key of All Keys."

Adding to its Masonic allure, its location is directly east of what was Mason's Island (now Roosevelt Island, named after Freemason Teddy Roosevelt). Better yet, the rock was chipped away and used as foundation stones by Masonic architect James Hoban for both the White House and the Capitol building, both of which had corner-stones laid by the Freemasons. And that means both buildings contain jigsaw puzzle pieces of the "Key of All Keys."

With understandable excitement, I persevered through one windy article or journal entry after another in my lone quest to decipher what I was convinced was one of the lost secrets of Freemasonry and the founding of Washington, D.C., itself.

I discovered a book called *The Royal Secret,* written in 1923 by Freemason I. Edward Clark, and in it an entire chapter was devoted to a very different "key of all keys." Clark writes, "*The swastika cross is the key of all keys, and a knowledge of the numerals of the Hebrew alphabet is necessary to unravel the Mysteries attached therein.*"[5]

Terrific. Somehow I hadn't anticipated a Hebrew swastika. It was another small setback, even if the swastika in 1923 hadn't yet acquired its creepier, more sinister reputation. Still, I knew there had to be a symbolic explanation, and I knew I was on the trail of a Very Big Secret, one that even Dan Brown hadn't uncovered.

That is, until I read Wilhelmus Bogart Bryan's *History of the National Capital*, written in 1914.[6] He explained that it was simply a variation of the phrase "quay of all quays." I remembered then that, on vacation in the Bahamas, I saw the local residents scoffing at tourists for their pronunciation of the word *quay*—islanders always pronounce it "key," like the Florida Keys.

So, after weeks of research and pondering and searching for an occult meaning behind an intriguing and obscure reference, it turned out to be just a very big rock that was a really good place to tie up your boat.

Or as Freud famously said, sometimes a cigar is just a cigar.

CHAPTER 1

Origin of the Freemasons

ᑕᚱᚱᒋᚱᗒ ᗒᑕ >ᑎᗒ ᑕᚱᗒᗒᒋᒑᐂᑕᗒᐂ

Maybe you've heard of the Freemasons before, or perhaps Dan Brown's *The Lost Symbol* is your first encounter with them. Perhaps your father or grandfather, or maybe a teacher or co-worker, was a Mason. Possibly you heard the term in the movie *National Treasure*, or you drive past a Masonic lodge every day. You might have seen their widely recognized symbol—the square and compass, usually with a *G* in the center—on a building or a cornerstone, on a sign as you drive into town, on a license plate, on a headstone in a graveyard, or on someone's ring.

Freemasonry is the world's largest, oldest, and most well-known fraternal organization. Masonry teaches lessons of social and moral virtues based on the symbolism of the tools and language of the ancient building trade, using the design and construction of a structure as a symbol for building character in men. Mythically descended from the builders of King Solomon's Temple in Jerusalem, Freemasonry is believed to have developed from the craft guilds of European stonemasons who built castles and cathedrals during the Middle Ages. Masons are obliged to practice brotherly love, mutual assistance, equality, secrecy, and trust among themselves.

Freemasonry is often described as a "secret society," even though the fraternity doesn't think of itself that way. Certainly in the United States and Canada, the existence of Freemasonry's buildings, members, and charities are no secret; they can easily be spotted on signs, in phone books, and on the Internet. In this part of the world, Masons commonly wear rings with Masonic symbols (most prominently, the square and compass) and have license plates on their cars identifying themselves as members. In other parts of the world, Freemasonry is not so open, and anti-Masons, or anyone suspicious of a locked door, often use Masonic secrecy as a stick with which to whack the fraternity. As a rule, the more oppressive the government, the less welcome the Freemasons, it seems. Hitler put them in the death camps; his motto was "All Jews Freemasons, all Freemasons Jews." There are still many countries today where being a Freemason can get you thrown into prison, or worse.

This chapter will consider the origin of the Freemasons, Masonic secrecy, and what Dan Brown got right and wrong about them in *The Lost Symbol*. In order to understand them, it's useful to explain what Freemasonry is, and to examine the roots of Masons' practices.

Defining Freemasonry

Today, there are at least 3 million Freemasons worldwide, including 1.5 million in the United States, and there are thousands of local Masonic lodges to be found around the globe. There is no national or international governing organization for Freemasonry. In North America and Australia, each state or province has its own organization, called a grand lodge, that claims "sovereignty" over the lodges in its territory. Outside of North America and Australia, most countries have their own governing grand lodge. There are agreements between these grand lodges that allow visitation and recognition between each others' members, often using the term "regular."

A closely related Masonic organization is the predominantly African-American Prince Hall Affiliated (PHA) group of grand lodges. The organization is named after Prince Hall, a prominent free black man from Boston who started a lodge in 1775. There are some 300,000 Prince Hall Masons in the U.S. and other countries around the world.

There are also competing organizations that are not considered regular or recognized by the mainstream grand lodges and frequently cause confusion both inside and outside of the fraternity.

Freemasonry initiates its members using three ceremonial rituals, referred to as *degrees*: the Entered Apprentice, the Fellow Craft, and the Master Mason. Regardless of any other Masonic organization a Freemason may join in his lifetime, and no matter how any other organization may describe or number their degrees, there is no degree of higher rank or importance in Freemasonry than the 3° Master Mason.

Freemasonry is based on the belief that each man can make a difference in the world by improving himself. It's not a religion, but it encourages its members to have a strong and active faith in the religion of their choice. It's not a service club, but it encourages individual Masons to take part in improving their communities. It's not a charity, but it teaches Masons to give back to society by being charitable. Yet, Freemasonry forbids the discussion in Masonic meetings of religion, creeds, politics or other topics likely to excite personal animosities.

Medieval Origins

There are lots of competing theories about the beginnings of the modern Freemason fraternity. Some are more fanciful than others, and some are downright ridiculous. Many of the more mythical theories arose during the Romantic period in the nineteenth century. The most popular of these explanations ties the Freemasons to the ancient monastic order of the Knights Templar, and there are a few interesting books, particularly *Born in Blood* by John Robinson, that make some compelling arguments for that case. However, most modern scholars follow the trail of the stonemason guilds of the Middle Ages.

Medieval stonemasons in the Christian West claimed that their trade guilds began with the great construction projects of the Bible, like the Tower of Babel and Solomon's Temple in order to give themselves a long, proud heritage and a more sacred-sounding pedigree. Early English documents purport that stonemasons were organized into guilds in that country at York in A.D. 926 by Athelstan.[1]

The Regius Manuscript, in the British Museum in London, is the earliest surviving record of a code of rules for the conduct of the stonemasons in England. It was written in A.D. 1390, but most historians agree that it was probably copied from an earlier source. It described rules for membership, a moral code, standards of workmanship, and the desire for a strong bond of close friendship among the members. The organization and structure for modern Freemasonry can be traced to this document, either by evolution or imitation—no one knows for certain.

The principal reason for the formation of the guilds was to teach new men the skills necessary to construct the castles, bridges, and cathedrals of the medieval period and to enforce high standards of workmanship. These skills and standards were the original secrets of the masons, and they were guarded fiercely. Keeping trade secrets among only the best craftsmen assured a higher price for their services. Apprentices began as young as age twelve and were indentured to a Master mason for up to seven years. After three years, they went through an initiation ceremony. They were given certain signs of recognition to identify themselves as a stonemason's apprentice, and they were granted permission to have their own *mark*, a small symbol carved into a stone to identify it as their own work. After they completed their seven years of service, they became a Fellow of the Craft (what we would now call a *journeyman*), and in time, with more experience, they graduated to the level of a Master mason, who was qualified to teach others. Master masons were in possession of the Master's *word* and *grip*, secret methods these master workmen used to recognize each other. It was a simple way to quickly identify themselves as trained members of the guild, even on worksites far from home; the word and grip were their calling cards.

The Catholic Church was the overwhelming religious influence in Europe by the turn of the first millennium. The Gothic cathedrals were certainly designed as massive symbols of the Church's power, but they also were created as places where the congregation could learn about religion through symbolism. In fact, the churches themselves were symbolic in their very design. The classic Gothic cathedral floor plans were arranged in the shape of a cross, and the buildings soared to unparalleled heights so the individual would feel as if he or she was lifted up in the presence of an all-powerful God. The common people were illiterate, so the stained-glass windows and stone carvings through-out the church were developed to pictorially tell stories from the Bible. The designers of the cathedrals were often visionary bishops, priests, or abbots, but skilled laborers were needed to do the exacting work of translating the fanciful designs into buildings that have last-ed ten centuries or more. To the common folk, the ability of Master masons to send these massive blocks of stone spiraling up toward heaven seemed to be nearly magical. These were the true secrets of the original stonemasons, and this was the reason highly confidential recognition signs were so important. Master masons had achieved a unique status in medieval Europe. They were not nobility, nor did they possess the formal education of the rising legal and priestly class-es, which moved in the orbit of the nobility. But they possessed the Knowledge, the secrets of building these magnificent cathedrals for the glory of God, and thus had achieved a position of great respect in the eyes of these two higher classes. These secrets, which granted such power and prestige, had to be kept concealed at all costs.

From Operative to Speculative Masonry

Beginning in the 1640s, records appeared showing that English and Scottish Masonic lodges began to admit honorary members into their ranks who were not workers in stone. These men were called *admit-ted* or *accepted* Masons, and this is the beginning of the change in Masonry from an "operative" guild that created buildings to a "spec-ulative" philosophical and social organization.

For a variety of reasons, it became the fashion for noblemen to seek admittance to the guilds of the Master masons, turning the usual direction of social climbing upside-down. Based on letters and jour-nals of this period, which was the dawn of the Age of Enlightenment, one of the reasons may have been that many educated young men of the high and petty nobility began to believe that there was something more important than being a man of the blood, and this was to be a man of reason. It was the catchword of the age. And of course, once the nobility joined in, everyone wanted a place at the table.

Besides, guilds, clubs, brotherhoods, and reading circles had become all the fashion. In 1660, some of the most respected men of science from across Britain had met and formed the *College for the Promoting of Physico-Mathematicall Experimentall Learning*, better known as the Royal Society. Based in London, this was a place where philosophers, scientists, and scholars could meet and discuss their latest theories. Royal Society members like Robert Moray, Elias Ashmole, and Dr. Jean-Theophilus Desaguliers also became speculative Freemasons. This new, speculative Freemasonry became an informal forum for discussion of the new sciences and philosophies of the Age of Reason, over a good meal and not a few drinks.

By the late 1600s, these "accepted" Masons saw in medieval Masonry the ideal symbolism for building character in men. Much like the cathedrals themselves, it was seen as a strong, well-balanced structure, built with the combined, knowledgeable assistance of many like-minded men, and ultimately dedicated to God. This concept was appealing for men who might have been free-thinkers who wanted to throw off the shackles of outmoded Church convention but were rarely out-and-out atheists. Masonry was also an attractive metaphor to the Enlightenment mind, because these stonemasons were equals who rose in knowledge through plateaus of understanding, using the rational sciences to build monuments to faith.

This new group of scientific and philosophical intellectuals transformed the Freemason guilds into something more modern and more symbolic, using their medieval predecessors as a model. The first official *grand lodge* was formed in London in 1717 by four speculative Masonic lodges. The symbolism of architecture became fundamental to the new fraternity, and the rituals and symbolism of Freemasonry placed the architect at its center. On a medieval cathedral project, the architect was a true, well-rounded intellectual. An architect had to know mathematics, geometry, physics, art, and even literature. In a way, he was a study in the classical liberal arts, or in other words, a Renaissance man. Freemasonry sought to instill these virtues and attributes in its members.

There was one more Enlightenment ideal that these men brought to the table: the separation of religion, not necessarily from the state but from hate. In regular Freemasonry, all candidates must have a belief in God. But by long-standing tradition, no Mason is allowed to discuss religion in the lodge. No Mason should even ask another Mason what faith he follows. Politics, too, are banned from the lodge and discouraged as a topic of conversation elsewhere except in the loftiest of terms. It's easy to understand why those who founded the Craft included this prohibition. These men of the early 1700s looked back on two centuries of bloody battles in Europe that were principally wars of religion. The English Civil War that their fathers and grandfathers had lived through pitted the Protestant Puritanism of Oliver Cromwell and the High Church Anglicanism of King Charles I. Throw in the Protestant revolt against the king by the rapidly growing Presbyterian church of Scotland and you've got a proper bloodbath over the issue of faith. Little wonder, then, that these men of reason and enlightenment wanted this kind of strife kept from the door of the lodge. Belief in God was essential because, in those days, it was assumed that if a man had no faith at all, he had no moral or ethical framework as well as no obligation to hold to the oaths of loyalty he took. But beyond this elemental belief, every man followed the dictates of his own conscience, dictates that were not to be questioned.

The hundred years following 1717 were the period of greatest expansion for the fraternity. Freemasonry circled the globe throughout the eighteenth century on the colonizing ships of the British, the French, and the Dutch. Benjamin Franklin, George Washington, John Hancock, Paul Revere, and many other Founding Fathers were among the first Masons in the United States.

Masonic Secrecy

The initiate exhaled, smiling inwardly as he gazed up at the unsuspecting gray-eyed man who had foolishly admitted him into this brotherhood's most secretive ranks.

—*The Lost Symbol*, page 5 [2]

Mal'akh, Dan Brown's villain in *The Lost Symbol*, believes a common misconception: that 33° Masons possess some great, secret knowledge that all other Masons are denied. Author Rex Hutchens, Past Grand Master of Arizona and a 33° Scottish Rite Mason, remarked after reading this passage, "I know men who have received the 33° for no greater service to the Fraternity than pouring coffee for twenty years and who know absolutely nothing of Masonry's history, philosophy, or symbolism. Much less are they made to feel a part of 'this brotherhood's most secretive ranks.'"[3]

In reality, there are more than 11,000 members of the Scottish Rite in the United States today who are 33° Masons, and they are hardly secretive about it.[4] Many wear 33° rings, and they are entitled in correspondence to be referred to as "Illustrious Brother." Some are elevated to a position of an "active" 33°, which places them in governing positions of the Rite, but most are in "honorary" positions. In any case, the 33° teaches no greater lessons and imparts no greater, deeper, or darker secrets than the other degrees of the Scottish Rite. Certainly not the secret to Life, the Universe, and Everything. If there really were 11,000 guys with the secret of the universe floating around, the world would be a very different place.

All of the "appendant bodies" of Freemasonry, the Scottish Rite, the York Rite, the Shrine, and many other groups are additional honors achievable by passing through fascinating rituals. But most Masons will tell you that nothing in any of these appendant societies is any "higher" in rank than the ultimate honor achieved by passing through the three ancient degrees and becoming a Master Mason.

Freemasonry does have secrets, but Masonic secrecy is one of the most misunderstood aspects of the fraternity. Freemasonry teaches its philosophy to its members through symbolism, and the notion of Masonic secrecy is itself a symbol—of honor.

It's not the "secrets" themselves that Masons are so concerned about revealing. But if a person can't be trusted to keep a simple secret like a password or a handshake, his word isn't really worth much. He is not considered an honorable person. At the time of Masonry's modern creation, in the early eighteenth century, men still fought duels over questions of honor. Calling someone a liar was a deadly insult that could get a man killed. And part of this personal honor was to be able to keep your word, as well as to keep a secret.

There are other secrets, of course, besides these modes of recognition. Some have to do with the specifics of Masonic rituals and ceremonies of initiation; others are more personal, and different for each Freemason. The central experience of Freemasonry, like many other fraternities and secretive societies, and even the Boy Scouts, is initiation. As in all initiation-based experiences in the world, the real secrets of Freemasonry are the effects its teachings and ceremonies have on the individual, and the way they are applied to his life.

> Freemasonry, I admit, has its secrets. It has secrets peculiar to itself, but of what do these principally consist? They consist of signs and tokens which serve as testimonials of character and qualifications, which are conferred after due instruction and examination.
>
> These are of no small value. They speak a universal language and are a passport to the support and attention of the world. They cannot be lost so long as memory retains its power. Let the possessor of them be expatriated, shipwrecked or imprisoned; let him be stripped of everything he has in the world, still their credentials remain, and are available for use as circumstances require.
>
> The good effects which they have produced are established by the incontestable facts of history. They have stayed the uplifted hand of the destroyer; they have subdued the rancor of malevolence and broken down the barriers of political animosity and sectarian alienation.

On the battlefield, in the solitudes of the uncultivated forest
or in the busy haunts of the crowded city, they have made men,
of the most hostile feelings and the most diversified conditions,
rush to the aid of each other with special joy and satisfaction
that they have been able to afford relief to a Brother Mason.

Attributed to Benjamin Franklin, 1778 [5]

Rarely has this thought been stated so eloquently. It is the noble aspect of freemasonry that, in the eye of conspiracy peddlers, has been reduced to something base. No, Masonic judges do *not* let off defendants who are Freemasons. Masonic cops don't even let them out of tickets; my driving record is clear proof of that, despite all the Masonic symbols all over my car. In American Masonic ritual, Masons are always enjoined to honor their nation and its laws. However, history is filled with stories of Freemasons on opposite sides in wartime aiding one another, even when the tradition of military officers presenting their swords in defeat had long passed. All Freemasons are brothers, and in Masonic philosophy, this fact stands as the truth in microcosm. The greater truth is that all men are brothers.

Dan Brown's novel tells a thrilling tale of trust, murder, betrayal, revenge, secrecy, and human transformation. That's Freemasonry in a nutshell. The central lessons taught to a Freemason are to "listen, learn, and be silent," and to govern his life by the cardinal virtues of justice, prudence, temperance (or restraint), fortitude, faith, hope, and charity. Masons are certainly not the only guys on the block to use these building blocks of moral character. The term *cardinal* is derived from the Latin *cardo*, meaning "hinge." The cardinal virtues are the hinges from which a moral life hangs and balances.

The way Masonry teaches its lessons is through rituals, or small morality plays, known as degrees. The Master Mason degree tells the tale of the building of King Solomon's Temple by way of a fictitious story of Hiram Abiff, "a widow's son." The Bible mentions Hiram (or Huram) in two passages:

I Kings 7:13-14: And king Solomon sent and fetched Hiram out of Tyre. He was a widow's son of the tribe of Naphtali, and his father was a man of Tyre, a worker in brass: and he was filled with wisdom, and understanding, and cunning to work all works in brass. And he came to king Solomon, and wrought all his work.

2 Chronicles 2:13-14: And now I have sent a skillful man, endued with understanding, of Huram, my father's,

The son of a woman of the daughters of Dan, and his father was a man of Tyre, skillful to work in gold and in silver, in bronze, in iron, in stone and in timber, in purple, in blue, and in fine linen, and in crimson; also to engrave any manner of engraving, and to devise every plan which shall be put to him, with thy skillful men and with the skillful men of my lord David thy father.

The Master Mason degree was developed in the 1720s and explains Hiram's role as the Master Architect of the Temple, who, as a Master Mason, possessed even greater secrets than the skilled Fellows of the Craft or journeymen. Each day, Hiram enters the temple to pray and to draw his designs for the workmen to accomplish on

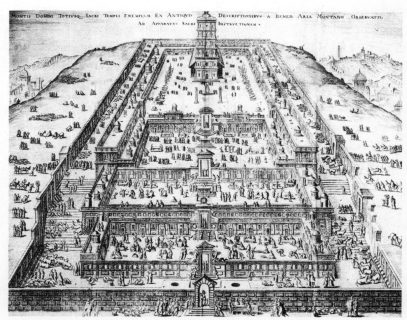

A sixteenth-century Spanish rendering of King Solomon's Temple in Jerusalem.

his "trestle board," or drawing board. Upon leaving one day, he is accosted by three of the temple's Fellow Craft, who are eager to discover the secrets of the Master Masons. Each threaten the Architect and attack him with their working tools.

Hiram dies without divulging the secrets he has vowed to protect, and the "word" of the Master Mason goes to the grave with him, in a lesson that teaches fidelity, honor and steadfastness in the face of death. Likewise, in Dan Brown's novel, Peter Solomon faces death at the hands of Mal'akh and refuses to divulge the secrets he has been entrusted with, even to save his life or the life of his sister.

The Wide World of Anti-Masonry

Some critics of Brown's book have snorted that one of the key plot points is generated by a ridiculous notion. The Central Intelligence Agency is involved in getting to the bottom of the disappearance of Peter Solomon and apprehending Mal'akh because of a terrible possibility: Mal'akh threatens to upload to YouTube a surreptitiously recorded video of a collection of high-ranking members of the government, all dressed in their Masonic regalia and performing the degree rituals. Robert Langdon and Peter Solomon watch "in horror" as the video clip unreels. Two Supreme Court justices, the secretary of defense, the speaker of the House (not Nancy Pelosi), the Senate majority leader, the secretary of Homeland Security, the director of the CIA, and the head of the Smithsonian all cluster calmly around the altar of the Scottish Rite's House of the Temple as a candidate is lowered into a coffin and, later, drinks wine out of a skull.

> Langdon could barely get his mind around what would happen if this video were made public. *No one would understand.* The government would be thrown into upheaval ... *The truth will be twisted*, Langdon knew. *As it always is with the Masons.*
>
> *The Lost Symbol*, page 437

Brown is correct when he says the truth is twisted with the Masons. Anti-Masons have never shrunk from deliberately misquoting ritual or Masonic authors, or simply fabricating stories, because Freemasons historically have not responded to critics. But the thought that the government of the United States would be turned on its ear by the revelation that high-ranking members were participating in Masonic ceremonies is a bit far-fetched. Then again, perhaps the skull business might make it onto the news.

American Freemasons are justifiably proud of the role Masons played in the founding and subsequent government of the U.S. Beginning with George Washington, fourteen presidents have been Masons, as were nine of the fifty-six signers of the Declaration of Independence and thirteen of the thirty-nine signers of the U.S. Constitution. The last Masonic president, as of 2009, was Gerald R. Ford, who died in 2006.

Actually, it wouldn't be surprising if Brown's book does even better in Europe than it does in the United States. That's because, while some Americans might feel that an uproar over Mal'akh's video is improbable, a European would probably not agree. In fact, it's rare for a major government shake-up to occur in Europe in which someone, somewhere, doesn't blame it on the Freemasons.

Britain, Spain, Italy, and France are all hotbeds of hostility to Freemasonry. For an American Mason, happily strolling the Champs Élysées, it can be disconcerting to pass the news kiosks on every corner and see the blaring headlines about "la conspiration de les francsmaçons" that decorate respectable French newsmagazines. Although President Jacques Chirac was not a Freemason, his twelve years as president were dogged by accusations that a small cabal of Freemasons was the real power behind the throne. The fact is, European readers would probably tremble at the possible political and social chaos that could be unleashed by the exposure of such a video.

In the United States, it's a bit different. During the 2004 presidential election season, it was widely reported that Republican candidate George W. Bush and Democratic challenger John Kerry were both members of the secretive Yale University society Skull and Bones. News reports, cable channel documentaries, blogs, and Amazon.com's nonfiction list all buzzed with lurid tales of the reputed rituals of Yale's exclusive Bonesmen: stealing skulls (allegedly including Indian chief Geronimo's), laying in coffins, being forced to confess their darkest sexual secrets, and blackmailing each other for high-powered government jobs. The CIA itself was reportedly created and staffed in the 1950s with many members of Skull and Bones. In fact, when Bush and Kerry were asked separately about their membership in the society, both blushed a little and replied that they were not allowed to speak of it. None of that "shocking news" stopped the presses, kicked either candidate to the curb, or disrupted the election.

However, outside of the United States, Masonophobia is very real and widespread. Freemasonry has been attacked all around the world for most of its 300-year lifespan because of the irrational fears of conspiracists who want simple answers and easily identifiable boogeymen to explain complex circumstances.

This isn't just ancient history. A Masonic lodge was bombed in Turkey as recently as 2004.[6] As this is being written, British and Italian Masons are fighting a series of draconian laws and ordinances that curtail their privacy and freedom.[7] In Britain, it is common for Masons who run for public office, or are involved in the judiciary or law enforcement, to be forced by local laws to "admit" their membership in the fraternity or sign a document swearing that they are not Freemasons. In Islamic countries that have Sharia laws based on a strict interpretation of the Qu'ran, Freemasonry is outlawed and is forced to operate in secrecy, if at all. Anti-Masonic laws are also common in many former Soviet satellite countries. Russia has only allowed Masonic lodges to reopen since the collapse of the Soviet system.

North American Masons are often shocked at the very different attitude toward the fraternity in other nations. Spain and France both have many anti-Masonic critics, so much so that my French brethren have warned me against open displays of Masonic jewelry in public. I made the mistake of posting a photograph of several Masonic friends at a dinner in Paris on my blog site several years ago. One of the men wrote me several months later asking me to remove his picture and name because he had been attacked professionally over his Masonic membership and passed over for an important international appointment because of it.

Governments aren't the only ones who get worked up over Masonry. The Freemasons have had a rather contentious relationship with the Catholic Church, which has issued several papal bulls and encyclicals against the fraternity over the last 300 years, despite the fact that hundreds of thousands of Freemasons are Catholics and Masonry remains popular in many predominantly Catholic countries. Condemnation of Freemasonry is a common thread in some denominations of Lutherans and Baptists as well, and in the evangelical Christian movement. And although Masonry has been open to Jews since the eighteenth century, apparently, there are a lot of folks out there who don't like the idea of Christians, Jews, and Muslims sitting side by side in a fraternity dedicated to brotherhood. In March 2006, a Pakistani-born Georgia Tech student, Syed Haris Ahmed, was arrested with an accomplice after taking video footage of the George Washington Masonic memorial in Alexandria, Virginia, which was passed along to alleged terrorists in London and Toronto.[8] Ahmed used the footage as a calling card to get himself recruited by al-Qaeda, hoping the group would bomb the building. He told the FBI he believed the Freemasons were "like the devil."

Freemasonry continues to evolve. It has always adapted to suit the needs and desires of its members, which is why throughout this book you will find disclaimers and seemingly evasive explanations and qualifiers about different parts of the world, different time periods, and different rituals. There is no single, worldwide governing authority for Freemasonry, which makes the "New World Order," the one-world Masonic government accusation made by many anti-Masons, so delusional.

Dan Brown's treatment of Freemasonry is unusual because Masonry has frequently been used as a negative force in the last thirty years of fiction references. *The Lost Symbol*, Katherine Kurtz's novel *Two Crowns for America*, and the film *National Treasure* are rare examples where Masons are seen as the "good guys," instead of criminals, deranged murderers, or Machiavellian political plotters. Dan Brown's even greater impact on Freemasonry has been the five-year-long rumor that Masons would be at the center of his sequel to *The Da Vinci Code*. That alone motivated publishers, television networks and filmmakers to create an avalanche of books and programs with largely positive and correct information about the fraternity. The result is that after more than twenty-five years of declining membership and vanishing from public memory, the Masons may be making a comeback, as a whole new generation discovers them.

CHAPTER 2

Masonic Rituals

⊐⎍∨⊏⊐⌐⌐ ⌐⌐><⌐⌐∨

Most non-Masons have an enormous curiosity about the most secret aspect of the fraternity: namely, the rituals that go on behind closed doors. In fact, discovering the details of the rituals, passwords, and other minutia of Masonry has been a game for some and a mania for others since the beginning. My own mother has been begging me for years to tell her whether she has "the Masonic handshake" right or not. She'll get nothing out of me.

The word *mystery* comes from the French word *mystère*, which originally meant any trade or craft during the Middle Ages. By the mid-1200s, merchant and craft guilds presented mystery plays based on stories of the Bible. The plays generally had something to do with whatever the guild specialized in: fishmongers might tell the story of Jonah and the Whale; bakers would present the Last Supper; pinners (nail makers) might stage the tale of Jesus's crucifixion; carpenters might present the story of Noah's Ark. The Masons often presented the story of the building of King Solomon's Temple.

The plays were performed on holy days in honor of the saints. They were put on by illiterate men and were learned by repeating the parts over and over until they were memorized. It's possible that this is where the use of dramatic ritual in initiations began to take form.

Even though the first grand lodge of Freemasons was officially established in London in 1717, a pamphlet was distributed in London in 1696 denouncing the Masons for their secret "Mischiefs and Evils." Various manuscripts exposing portions of the ritual started appearing some twenty years before that in England, Scotland,[1] and Ireland.[2] Some of these early *exposures*, as Masons refer to them, may simply have been memory aids written by Masons themselves, but others, like the widely circulated *Masonry Dissected* (1730) by Samuel Pritchard and *Illustrations of Masonry* by William Morgan (1826) were clearly designed to embarrass or enrage Masons by revealing their secrets. In many cases, however, the biggest purchasers of these popular publications were Freemasons themselves.

I have discussed Masonic secrecy in general terms in Chapter 1, but in this chapter I will focus on the secrecy surrounding the ritual itself.

One of the first things a new Entered Apprentice promises not to do is to "write, print, paint, stamp, stain, carve, hew, mark, or engrave" any of the secrets of the fraternity so non-Masons can read them. As a result, most of Masonic ritual ceremony is conducted from memory.

This practice, like many in Freemasonry, stems from its origins in the Middle Ages. In the medieval stonemason guilds, it was the custom for the Master to teach the apprentice the knowledge of his trade. This aspect of operative masonry was carried into speculative Freemasonry, but modern Masons weren't showing each other how to carve rocks anymore. Instead, they were passing along complex ritual, from mouth to ear, from one brother to the next.

Historians say that many of Shakespeare's plays weren't written down until after he had died; in order to do so, scribes copied down the words that the actors of the Globe Theatre had long ago memorized. However, for Masonic candidates who don't have the memory of a Shakespearean actor, this prohibition against writing down the ritual has been a heavy burden to bear. Sneaking written copies of sections of ritual for practice, along with a variety of other memory aids, is as old as Masonry itself.

The prohibition against writing down Masonic ritual may seem harsh, but there were reasons for this eccentric dictate. The most important one is that learning from a book is something a man experiences alone, but learning in regular sessions with a Mason forms a bond between members. These mentor-apprentice relationships often become the basis of lifelong friendships.

Another reason Masons keep their rituals secret is very simple: part of the power of the initiation experience comes from confronting the unknown. Initiation is an ordeal in which a person is tested, confronts a fear, succeeds at a quest, or passes a milestone. The Jewish bar mitzvah, Christian baptism, the Boy Scouts' Order of the Arrow ordeal, induction into a monastic order, military hazing—all of these share the common thread of marking a dramatic change in one's life, highlighted by a memorable, and sometimes life-altering, experience. Such an experience is spoiled if you read about it the night before on the Internet, or even trembling under the sheets with a flashlight.

The Masonic Degrees

There are three rituals that a Freemason must undergo to become a full member in the local Masonic lodge: the Entered Apprentice, Fellow Craft, and Master Mason ceremonies. These stages are called *degrees*, and each has its own specific ritual. As the member progresses, each ceremony becomes longer and more detailed presenting more of the overall story that is the central symbol of Masonic ritual: the building of King Solomon's Temple in Jerusalem. The fraternity uses the temple as an allegory for character building in men, and Freemasonry uses the tools and terminology of the stonemason's trade to teach its lessons.

In the prologue of *The Lost Symbol*, Brown describes Mal'akh receiving the 33° of the Scottish Rite, but it gets a little muddled by being conflated with a flashback to his original initiation night as an Entered Apprentice:

> As was tradition, he had begun this journey adorned in the ritualistic garb of a medieval heretic being led to the gallows, his loose-fitting shirt gaping open to reveal his pale chest, his left pant leg rolled up to the knee, and his right sleeve rolled up to the elbow. Around his neck hung a heavy rope noose—a "cable-tow" as the brethren called it.
>
> *The Lost Symbol*, page 3

A candidate for the first three degrees of Freemasonry is indeed blindfolded, or "hoodwinked" (from an archaic term meaning to cover the eyes). He is in darkness during his initiation so he cannot see the details of the lodge; this also heightens the awareness of his other senses and is a symbol of his lack of knowledge. The last words he hears before his eyes are uncovered are "Let there be light"—a term for knowledge, and thus enlightenment.

The initiate does actually have a rope around his neck called a "cable-tow," but it is not a noose, and it is never meant to represent an instrument of torture or death. However, this clearly hasn't always been the case. In the Dumfries-Kilwinning Manuscript No. 4 (c. 1700–1725), a series of questions and answers gives the origin of the practice a slightly edgier explanation than modern Masonic ritual:

> How were you brought in?
> Shamefully with a rope around my neck . . .
> Why a rope around your neck?
> To hang me if I should betray my trust.[3]

Its symbolic purpose is to be there to lead him out of the lodge if he should wish not to proceed with his initiation. The cable-tow takes on more significance in the two succeeding degrees as a demonstration of the invisible "tie that binds" brethren together. Interestingly, there is one place where this image of a blindfolded man with a rope around his neck appears that might be the source of Brown's interpretation of the ritual. Scotland's Rosslyn Chapel has intrigued Freemasons and a raft of others who believe it contains a plethora of secrets within its intricately carved stone walls, and it is the location of the finale of Brown's *The Da Vinci Code*. Some have perpetuated the legend that the medieval Knights Templar fled their persecution in France in 1307 and found sanctuary in Scotland, where they built Rosslyn Chapel to hide their treasure and then morphed into the Freemasons by the 1600s. This tale was largely the invention of Scottish Freemasons in the 1700s, who were less than enthused that London Masons were claiming to have a more "ancient," and somehow more legitimate, heritage than their Scottish brethren.[4] Innumerable books have come forth since the 1970s repeating this very old allegation, most notably John Robinson's *Born in Blood*, and Michael Baigent and Richard Leigh's *The Temple and the Lodge*.

The truth is that Rosslyn Chapel was built by William Sinclair (Scottish for St. Clair) beginning in 1440 as a private, family chapel that was intended to be part of a much larger cathedral, which was never constructed. The Sinclairs were indeed connected to the medieval Templar order. Henri Saint-Clair, First Earl of Roslin, fought in the First Crusade alongside Templar founders Godfroi de Bouillon and Hugues de Payens, and the Freemasons of Scotland invited William Sinclair to become Grand Master of Masons in 1736. But there is nothing at Rosslyn that proves the Templars transformed into the Freemasons.

Many researchers have peered squinty-eyed at the thousands of carvings in the little chapel, desperate to discover any authentic, specifically Masonic symbols. Put bluntly, there aren't any. Out of the literally hundreds of symbols that are used in Masonic ritual, lectures, and literature, not one of them appears in Rosslyn Chapel.

The only carving that can remotely be linked to Freemasonry is a small piece on the outside of the chapel, depicting a blindfolded man with a noose around his neck and an open Bible in his hand (or it's assumed to be a Bible—the image is far too weatherworn to tell) being led by what appears to be a hooded executioner. Some argue that this is clearly a medieval representation of an initiate for the Entered Apprentice degree, while others say it depicts an exe-

The alleged Entered Apprentice carving at Rosslyn Chapel.

cution, or even an illustration of "the blind leading the blind." But with no other specific Masonic images in the entire building, it's unlikely to be related to Freemasonry, no matter how much wishful thinkers may want it to be. Although there is no proof that Rosslyn's carving is Masonic, there is the remote possibility that seventeenth-century Scottish Masons may have been inspired by some of these carvings, or the practices they depict, in creating their own practices and legends, in just the same fashion that Dan Brown may have been.

Bloody Oaths

Each degree of Masonic ritual has a list of obligations the candidate promises to abide by, and each degree has a symbolic penalty that comes with it. In the Middle Ages, breaking a vow, oath, or what the French called a *parole*, was a far graver offense than modern folks can comprehend. English mariners took variations of these oaths during the fifteenth century, as did lawyers admitted to the bar in London during the sixteenth century. These early oaths—often alluding to death or dismemberment—actually grew out of court-mandated punishments during the Middle Ages. It was believed that an incomplete body could not rise from the dead, nor could a body buried in unconsecrated ground. Therefore, to be buried without all of your body parts ensured terrible condemnation in the hereafter.

The obligations taken by Freemasons have been the source of complaints for many years by critics who have taken the "bloody penalties" as a serious threat. Freemasons are told during every degree that the obligations they are about to take contain nothing that can conflict with their duty to God, their country, their neighbor, or themselves. There is no recorded evidence of any Freemason who has ever had his throat slit, his chest torn open, or his body disemboweled for telling a non-Mason how to give the secret handshake.

Over the years, as critics have objected to such oaths, Masonic jurisdictions have answered the criticism in different ways. In England, the oaths have been removed from the obligations altogether. In many

U.S. jurisdictions, they have been modified with a statement that they are only symbolic, or that these were the ancient penalties and are no longer enforced. The truth is, they never were. The only penalties in Freemasonry are reprimand, suspension, or expulsion from the fraternity.

Brown makes other errors in his descriptions of ritual, as well. For instance, the degree is portrayed as being presided over by someone referred to as the "Supreme Worshipful Master."[5] Nowhere in all of the Masonic degrees or appendant organizations is anyone referred to as a "Supreme Worshipful Master." The position roughly equivalent to the "president" in a Masonic lodge is referred to as the Worshipful Master, but he's not a "supreme" anything, and the term is not meant to imply that anyone worships him. I have held the position in two different lodges myself, and I assure you, nobody was worshipping me. It actually comes from the English tradition of referring to certain officials with a term of deep respect and honor, such as "the Worshipful Lord Mayor" (French Masons use the term "venerable" when referring to their lodge Masters). The proper title of the highest-ranking officer in the Scottish Rite is the Sovereign Grand Commander.

> *"May this wine I now drink become a deadly poison to me . . . should I ever knowingly or willfully violate my oath". . .* Steadying his hands, the initiate raised the skull to his mouth and felt his lips touch the dry bone. He closed his eyes and tipped the skull toward his mouth, drinking the wine in long, deep swallows. When the last drop was gone, he lowered the skull.[6]

The specific ceremony described by Brown in the prologue of *The Lost Symbol* was adapted from a sensationalized exposé, *Scotch Rite Masonry Illustrated*, published in 1887 by the Reverend John Blanchard. Blanchard's description of the 33° has been repeated by many anti-Masonic authors over the years, even though it is not accurate. In his description, not only do 33°s drink from skulls, the lodge room is strewn with skeletons, and the candidate has skeletons thrust upon him in scenes more reminiscent of nineteenth-century Odd Fellows rituals.

Brown's use of Blanchard's imagery is surprising in light of the glowing comments he has made about Masonry since the publication of *The Lost Symbol*. In a recent interview with the Associated Press, he said:

> I have enormous respect for the Masons. In the most funda-
> mental terms, with different cultures killing each other over
> whose version of God is correct, here is a worldwide organiza-
> tion that essentially says, "We don't care what you call God, or
> what you think about God, only that you believe in a god and
> let's all stand together as brothers and look in the same direc-
> tion."[7]

It could just be that Brown was taking poetic license and making Masonic ritual seem spookier than it is. Or he could be intentionally avoiding the exact wording out of respect, so as to not reveal the precise details of Masonic ceremonies. Or he simply got them wrong.

CHAPTER 3

Art, Codes, and the Cover of *The Lost Symbol*

⊐⌐>, ⌐⊑⊐⊃∨, ⊐⊐⊐ >⊓⊐ ⌐⊑∧⊐⌐
⊑⊏ >⊓⊐ ⌐⊑∨> ∨<⊐⊔⊑⊏

Nothing is concealed from the wise and sensible, while the
unbelieving and unworthy cannot learn the secrets.
HEINRICH CORNELIUS AGRIPPA

The covers of Dan Brown's most recent novels, *The Da Vinci Code*
and *The Lost Symbol*, have both contained many images, layers, and
puzzles, and Brown packs his narrative with codes, puzzles, and artwork, too. Sometimes he explains them, sometimes he doesn't. In this
chapter, I analyze an assortment of these elements that appear in *The
Lost Symbol* and on its cover.

*Caution: There are serious spoilers ahead. If you have any inten-
tion of trying to find the puzzles and their solutions on your own, skip
the next three pages!*

Masonic Codes

The cover of the U.S. hardback version of Brown's latest book features
several sets of mysterious codes to unlock. The most prominent is a
series of coded letters on the back.

⊐⊑⊑ ⌐⌐⊐⊐> >⌐<>⊓∨
⊔⊐⌐⊏ ⊐∨ ⊔⊑⊐∨⌐⊓⊐⊐⌐⊐∨

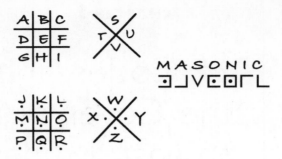

A Masonic cipher code, as described in The Lost Symbol.

As Dan Brown describes in *The Lost Symbol*, a Masonic code has been used for several hundred years. Its origin is in the Royal Arch degrees of the York Rite. In the course of the degree, the candidate is taught the cipher so he will be able to decode the message, which is the key to the ineffable name of God, the Tetragrammaton. The code is deciphered by taking the alphabet and placing it in a tic-tac-toe pattern, then using vertical and horizontal lines and dots to replace the corresponding letters. Some confusion has occurred over the years among those who sought to decipher the code, as the keys in England differ from the ones in the United States. This is sometimes referred to as a "pigpen cipher" because the pattern resembles an old-fashioned pig-pen from above.

The coded message translates as "All great truths begin as blasphemies." The phrase comes from George Bernard Shaw's play, *Annajanska, the Bolshevik Empress* (1919).

Numbers and Letters

Faintly printed in red around the cover of the book are a series of letters and numbers. These were designed as part of a puzzle and a contest by Brown and his publisher. The combinations were *A2, B1, C2, D7, E8, F2, G9, H5, I1, J5*. They were deciphered by arranging the numbers in order of the letters, which revealed a telephone number:

212-782-9515. The first thirty-three people who called the number won an autographed copy of the book, and a recorded telephone message told them how to claim their prize.

Once the copies were all won, the recording was changed to a monotone voice, recorded backwards. When played in reverse, it repeats the pseudo-Latin phrase chanted by Mal'akh in the novel, "*Verbum significatium, verbum omnificum, verbum perdo.*"

In *The Lost Symbol*, the *verbum significatium* is explained by a student of Peter Solomon's:

> According to legend, the sages who encrypted the Ancient Mysteries long ago left behind a *key* of sorts . . . a *password* that could be used to unlock the encrypted secrets. This magical password—known as the *verbum significatium*—is said to hold the power to lift the darkness and unlock the Ancient Mysteries, opening them to all human understanding.[1]

The explanation goes on that the word waits patiently underground for a pivotal moment in history when the world simply won't be able to survive another day without truth, wisdom, and knowledge. At that point it will be revealed, and mankind will live in a wonderful new world of enlightenment. While this sounds like a standard fantasy about the so-called Ancient Mysteries, this particular phrasing is a complete invention of Brown's. And it's lousy Latin, too. With a stretch, "*Verbum significatium, verbum omnificum, verbum perdo*" sort of means "password, almighty word, word of destruction."

Another puzzle on the cover involved a "magic square."

```
Y  U  O  E
M  S  T  D
I  I  N  H
R  E  K  Y
```

Using the methods described in the book, it translates into the phrase, "*Your mind is the key.*"

Two strings of symbols, across the top and bottom of the cover printed in dark gray, are made up of alchemical symbols.

After investigating them and peering into their meanings and the order they appear in, they seem to be nothing more than an artistic element: using the font "Alchemy A," designed by Denise Kohler and sold by Deniart Systems, they are simply typed in the alphabetical order of abcdefghijklmnopqrstuvwxyz.

In 1514, the German artist Albrecht Dürer (1471–1528) created what may be one of the most discussed works of art you've never heard of, at least until Dan Brown told you about it. The copper engraving, *Melencolia I*, contains so much unexplained symbolism that art critics, alchemists, philosophers, and even Freemasons have been poring over it for nearly five centuries attempting to decipher its enigmatic imagery.

Albrecht Dürer's Melencolia I *(1514).*

The engraving depicts what appears to be a dejected angel, staring into the distance, with a set of compasses in her hand and her right elbow resting on a closed book. Above her is an hourglass, about midway through running out, and a bell. At her feet are the tools of a woodworker: nails, a saw, a wood plane, along with a set of tongs. She has a set of keys hanging around her waist. There is also a small satchel, looking not unlike a coin purse, and a sphere, about bowling-ball sized. There is a dog curled up on the floor, with what appears to be a censer next to it. On the angel's right is a small winged cherub, not looking too happy either. The cherub sits on a round millstone and is next to a ladder. Above its head is a set of scales. On the left of the frame is what appears to be a multifaceted stone, smoothly finished into a complex shape known as a polyhedron with a vague image of a skull on one surface, and a hammer on the floor. Behind the stone is a fire-stoked crucible, used for melting metals, a common practice of alchemists. In the background, there is a seaside scene, with a blazing star (or sun, or even Halley's Comet) and a rainbow. Flying through the sky is a bat or a winged dragon, or perhaps even a demon, unfurling a banner that says "Melencolia I."

Prominent in the image is something Dan Brown uses as a plot device in *The Lost Symbol*: a 4x4 magic square (sometimes called a Jupiter square). It depicts four columns and four rows of numbers that add up to *34* in all directions, and to reinforce this, the hourglass above the square has a pointer that is set between *3* and *4*. In the bottom row, the numbers *15* and *14*—the year the engraving was made—appear next to each other. In the novel, Robert Langdon figures out that Dürer's image is important to his quest based on seeing the clue "1514 AD." Indeed, near the bottom right corner, the year 1514 appears again, over Dürer's distinctive "AD" monogram.

Time has proved that it is impossible to discern all of Dürer's intended meaning. Thousands of papers and well over a hundred books have attempted to put into words what the artist was attempting to communicate.

Some Freemasons have a tendency to believe that any ancient painting or picture that depicts a square or a set of compasses, especially if a geometric shape is involved, must be symbolic of the Craft. In H. L. Haywood's revision of Albert Mackey's *Encyclopedia of Freemasonry*, published in 1946, a long article featuring analysis by W. P. Tuckerman suggests that Dürer was obviously a Freemason in Nuremburg. According to Tuckerman, the compasses and the stone clearly depict Freemasonry, and the keys portray Masonic secrecy. The dog was a common Dürer symbol for the Church; which is why he would sometimes depict dogs lurking around kings' thrones. So, Tuckerman explains, when the priestly order "disregards its duty and, like the dog here, falls asleep, it belongs among the discarded tools and gives the laity who constitute the Masonic fraternity the right to open communication with the Most High without clerical mediation."[2]

Of course, Dürer was a painter and an engraver, not a stonemason. And he died in Germany in 1528, a century before anything approaching modern Freemasonry took form in Scotland, and 189 years before the formation of the first real Grand Lodge in London in 1717.

Dürer did have a fascination with mathematics, geometry, and physiognomy, which are obvious in the details of his work. His first breakthrough project was a series of sixteen etchings of scenes of the Apocalypse in 1498. Based on the biblical account in Revelation, it rapidly gained popularity because of a widespread fear that the world would end in A.D. 1500.

More Magic Squares

Magic squares can be found in the ruins of ancient Egypt. They appeared in China in 650 B.C., and were found in India by Arab and Persian mathematicians a thousand years later. More than just a mathematical mind game, they have been used through the ages as talismans, and cosmic significance has been attached to them.

As in Dürer's *Melencolia I*, and as Dan Brown discusses in *The Lost Symbol*, a magic square is a grid of numbers in which the rows and columns add up to the same sum. In Dürer's case, he went so far as to make the diagonal numbers, and even the corners all add up to 34, too.

In A.D. 1510, a German magician and occultist named Heinrich Cornelius Agrippa (1486–1535) drafted his famous work, *De occulta philosophia libri tres* (*Three Books Concerning Occult Philosophy*). If you have the slightest interest in Western magic and esoteric traditions, his books should be at the top of your reading list. Agrippa argued that practical magic was not incompatible with Christianity, and the three books outline elemental, celestial, and intellectual magic. He pulled together astrology, alchemy, numerology, Kabbalistic thought, and Greek and Hebrew mysticism and philosophy, and even managed to be the first to perpetuate the legend that the Knights Templar were practicing witchcraft. He believed that practical magic, which had descended from ancient practitioners, had become tainted by medieval witches, enchanters, and other dabblers in superstition. His hope was to "reform" magic and place it into the hands of a few learned wise men who would use their power for good and to improve society, not just to turn miscreant teenagers into newts.

Agrippa included in his work a series of magic squares that were connected to the seven planets known at the time:

Saturn = 15

4	9	2
3	5	7
8	1	6

Jupiter = 34

4	14	15	1
9	7	6	12
5	11	10	8
16	2	3	13

Mars = 65

11	24	7	20	3
4	12	25	8	16
17	5	13	21	9
10	18	1	14	22
23	6	19	2	15

Sol = 111

6	32	3	34	35	1
7	11	27	28	8	30
19	14	16	15	23	24
18	20	22	21	17	13
25	29	10	9	26	12
36	5	33	4	2	31

Venus = 175

22	47	16	41	10	35	4
5	23	48	17	42	11	29
30	6	24	49	18	36	12
13	31	7	25	43	19	37
38	14	32	1	26	44	20
21	39	8	33	2	27	45
46	15	40	9	34	3	28

Mercury = 260

8	58	59	5	4	62	63	1
49	15	14	52	53	11	10	56
41	23	22	44	45	19	18	48
32	34	35	29	28	38	39	25
40	26	27	37	36	30	31	33
17	47	46	20	21	43	42	24
9	55	54	12	13	51	50	16
64	2	3	61	60	6	7	57

Luna = 369

37	78	29	70	21	62	13	54	5
6	38	79	30	71	22	63	14	46
47	7	39	80	31	72	23	55	15
16	48	8	40	81	32	64	24	56
57	17	49	9	41	73	33	65	25
26	58	18	50	1	42	74	34	66
67	27	59	10	51	2	43	75	35
36	68	19	60	11	52	3	44	76
77	28	69	20	61	12	53	4	45

Agrippa's magic squares, referred to in some texts as Kameas, were used as patterns to play the sort of word games used in *The Lost Symbol* to create incantations for magic spells, or to form talismans against spells. Remember that Brown was originally going to call his novel *The Solomon Key*. That title not only echoes the name of Peter and Katherine Solomon as plot points, it is also derived from a late medieval text called *The Key of Solomon*, which appeared in Europe in the late 1300s. Purportedly written originally by King Solomon in 1000 B.C., it is a book of spells and ritual magic, known as a *grimoire*, and it includes a famous magic square, known as the Sator Square, Instead of numbers, it uses letters to create a palindrome (letters that spell the same word forward or backward) in Latin. The words SATOR, AREPO, TENET, OPERA, and ROTAS are placed in a 5x5 square.

S	A	**T**	O	R
A	R	**E**	P	O
T	**E**	**N**	**E**	**T**
O	P	**E**	R	A
R	O	**T**	A	S

A general translation of the words is "*The sower Arepo holds the wheels with effort*" but the phrase itself doesn't communicate the true meaning of the square. The Sator Square appeared well before the Middle Ages and was even found on the walls of a building in Pompeii and on other Roman ruins. Some have theorized that it was a sign used by early Christians to show their secret presence in towns where they might be persecuted by authorities. Later explanations attached the words used in the square to the names of the nails used to crucify Christ.

Of particular interest to Freemasons, Christians, and interpreters of *The Lost Symbol*, there is also a magic square that adds up to the number 33. It appears on the exterior of La Sagrada Familia Cathedral in Barcelona, Spain, and was created in 1972 by the Spanish sculptor Josep Maria Subirachs as part of a facade known as "The Passion."

1	14	14	4
11	7	6	9
8	10	10	5
13	2	3	15

Unfortunately, Subirachs cheated by duplicating numbers in order to get the number 33, and to closely match Dürer's square in *Melencolia I*. The number 33 appears to present an insurmountable problem of not being divisible by 4, unless one of the numbers in the square is 0.

The American Zeus

In *The Lost Symbol*, Robert Langdon reminds CIA Director Sato that the dismembered hand of Peter Solomon is not the first to point a finger at the Apotheosis fresco in the ceiling of the Capitol rotunda. He is referring to a statue of George Washington as the god Zeus.

Thomas Jefferson referred to the men who drafted the Constitution as an "assembly of demigods," so it was hardly a surprise when Congress decided to immortalize George Washington in a similarly magisterial fashion. Greek symbolism was much admired in the Federal City, so it seemed like a roaring good idea to depict the president as a mythical Greek god. In 1832, the sculptor Horatio Greenough was commissioned by Congress to create the ultimate statue of the hero of the Revolution and father of the country, which was to be placed in the rotunda of the Capitol.

What got delivered eight years later was a representation of George sitting with his lower extremities wrapped in a toga and his torso naked as a proverbial jaybird. Greenough patterned the image after a classical statue of the Greek god Zeus at Olympia, one of the Seven Wonders of the Ancient World. The statue, installed in the rotunda in 1842, was greeted with a chorus of derision. No one had ever really thought of George Washington being naked before. In fact, Nathaniel Hawthorne summed up the public sentiment when he said, "I imagine he was born with his clothes on, and his hair powdered, and made a stately bow on his first appearance in the world."[3] Others put it more bluntly, saying it looked like the president was emerging from a long soak in a bathtub and reaching for a towel.

Equally distressing, while it was not quite as big as the original forty-foot statue of Zeus carved by Phidias in 456 B.C., from which it was copied, it sure weighed like it, tipping the scales at more than twenty tons. After a year in its designated location, it was determined to be too heavy and dangerous to the floor over the underground crypt that had originally been designed for Washington's body, so the huge, expensive embarrassment was moved to the great outdoors. When the weather finally began to damage the carving, it was hauled off to the

Smithsonian's National Museum of American History, where it can now be seen giving a solemn Olympian blessing to an escalator.

Washington sits on a throne, its panels containing the image of Helios, one of Zeus's innumerable sons, carrying the sun across the sky on a horse-drawn chariot. The other side of the throne shows the image of Zeus's other children. The baby Hercules and his twin brother Iphicles are shown in their crib. Their mother Hera became so enraged when she discovered Zeus had fathered Hercules by a mortal woman that she threw a snake into their crib. The infant Hercules is shown killing the snake with his bare hands. A five-pointed star—an upside-down pentagram—is shown over the head of Hercules, with the bottom point of the star touching his head.

Fringe author David Icke has claimed that the statue of

George Washington as the American Zeus.

Washington bears a striking resemblance in its pose to the famous illustration of Baphomet drawn by French occultist Eliphas Lévi. In both figures, the right arm points skyward and the left points downward in a manner reminiscent of the alchemical phrase, "As above, so below." Therefore, Icke suggests, Washington's statue illustrates that he is somehow an evil incarnation of Lévi's occult imagery. The drawing was made for Lévi's *Dogme et rituel de la haute magie*. Unfortunately for Icke's theory, the book appeared in 1855, fifteen years after the Greenough statue was completed. (Of course, Icke also believes Queen Elizabeth II is a reptilian space alien.) There is another explanation for Washington's odd posture in this statue. The original design of the Washington Monument by Robert Mills was supposed to have been a Greco-Roman temple, topped by a sculpture of

Eliphas Lévi's illustration of Baphomet, from Dogme et rituel de la haute magie *(1855).*

Washington in a chariot pulled by six horses. Greenough's statue looks strikingly similar to the posture of Washington in Mills's conceptual drawing. The outstretched hand that holds a sword might have actually been holding the reins of the chariot. It's possible that Greenough designed the statue as a sample to get the entire commission of Washington, chariot and horses and all, for the monument. Fortunately, cooler heads prevailed, and a more monumental, but more austere, design was chosen for the memorial.

On the other hand, maybe there is a far simpler explanation of the odd posture. In ancient Rome, former consul Lucius Quinctius Cincinnatus was working on his farm when word was delivered to him that he had been appointed dictator in order to repel an invasion. The sitting consul, Minucius, was under siege by the Volscians and the Aequi. Cincinnatus put down his plow and took up the sword. In just sixteen days, he took control of the army, freed Minucius, and repelled Rome's enemies. He then went back home and again took up the plow.

George Washington was often referred to as the American Cincinnatus, because as soon as the British surrendered at Yorktown, he went home to his farm. Factions across the country offered him every kind of honor and position, including the Freemasons, who wanted him to become the first Grand Master for a new Grand Lodge of the United States. If he had wanted to become America's first Caesar, the dictatorship might very well have been handed to him. After his election to two terms as president, he could have served in the position for the rest of his life. But Washington preferred to return to Mount Vernon and take up the plow.

The Greenough statue could just as easily show Washington, not as a god nor as Baphomet, but as Cincinnatus, the retiring consul, handing his sword back to the people. And maybe asking for his clothes.

Kryptos

Just outside Washington, D.C., one of the world's most enigmatic sculptures resides in front of the Central Intelligence Agency's headquarters in McLean, Virginia. It is mentioned on the very first page of *The Lost Symbol* as part of Brown's disclaimer that the sculpture really does exist, and it pops up throughout the story as something of a meaningless red herring to the plot.

In 1990, artist James Sanborn erected the sculpture, entitled Kryptos (the Greek word for hidden), in the northwest corner of the courtyard of the CIA's new building, right in the path of America's top-secret code breakers, challenging them—or anyone else—to decipher its message.

The whole sculpture is designed to be a microcosm of secret codes. As you approach the sculpture, it begins with two red granite and copper pieces that appear to be pages sprouting out of the sidewalk. These first copper "pages" are inscribed with Morse code and ancient ciphers. A magnetized lodestone with a compass rose inscribed on it is embedded in the walk.

Across a reflecting pool stands the centerpiece of the work, and the conversation piece that has caused more than its share of controversy. A large column of petrified wood appears to support a tall scroll of copper made to resemble a roll of paper covered with letters in seemingly nonsensical order. The letters make up a vast code of nearly 1,800 figures divided into four sections.

The first two sections are a table for encrypting and deciphering code using a method developed by sixteenth-century French cryptographer Blaise de Vigenère, whose idea was to substitute letters in a message by shifting letters in the alphabet forward or backward in order, using a predetermined key. Sanborn figured the code would be broken in days or weeks, yet the first three sections took nine years to decipher. Of the four sections of messages, three have been decoded over the years. (The spelling errors in the messages that follow are part of the decoding.) The first is a poetic message from the artist himself:

> Between subtle shading and the absence of light lies the nuance of iqlusion.

The second is a tantalizing message for treasure hunters:

> It was totally invisible. How's that possible? They used the earth's magnetic field. x The information was gathered and trans-mitted undergruund to an unknown location. x Does langley know about this? They should: it's buried out there somewhere. x Who knows the exact location? Only WW. This was his last message. x Thirty eight degrees fifty seven minutes six point five seconds north, seventy seven degrees eight minutes forty four seconds west. Layer two.

The third section is drawn from explorer Howard Carter's diary describing the opening of King Tutankhamen's tomb in Egypt in 1922:

> Slowly, desparatly slowly, the remains of passage debris that encumbered the lower part of the doorway was removed. With trembling hands I made a tiny breach in the upper left-hand cor-ner. And then, widening the hole a little, I inserted the candle and peered in. The hot air escaping from the chamber caused the flame to flicker, but presently details of the room within emerged from the mist. x Can you see anything? q

The fourth and final section consists of ninety-seven characters:

> OBKR
> UOXOGHULBSOLIFBBWFLRVQQPRNGKSSO
> TWTQSJQSSEKZZWATJKLUDIAWINFBNYP
> VTTMZFPKWGDKZXTJCDIGKUHUAUEKCAR

Sanborn gave a copy of the solution to the code and the riddle it contains to then-CIA Director William Webster, and it has been passed along to each succeeding CIA director since then. It is, in fact, to Webster that the line "Who knows the exact location? Only WW." refers.

The original dust jacket of the U.S. hardback edition of Dan Brown's book, *The Da Vinci Code*, contains two references to the Kryptos sculpture. In the artwork depicting a tear in a piece of parchment are the words "Only WW knows." On the back cover, latitude and longitude coordinates appear vertically in red. They are the coordinates from the second section of the Kryptos message, with one degree digit changed. It seems to point to the opposite corner of the same courtyard where the sculpture is placed. When Brown was questioned about the text, he replied, "The discrepancy is intentional."[4]

Would-be code breakers and Washington sightseers who wish to see the sculpture in person will be disappointed; there is no public access to the CIA's property. The simple act of driving up to the main gate to ask questions is considered trespassing, and they are very serious about it. I can verify this personally, as I was detained at the gate by very unsympathetic, and well-armed, guards when I asked the perfectly idiotic question, "Hey, can I come on the grounds and take some photographs?" The CIA is aware of public interest in the sculpture and its code and has set up an official Web page about Kryptos.[5]

In 2006, Sanborn sheepishly revealed that he had made a mistake in the original code on Kryptos. He had removed a single X from the sculpture's text for artistic reasons, which had the effect of rendering the accepted solution to part two incorrect. The characters that had been deciphered as "IDBYROWS" should have decoded as "XLAYERTWO" Apparently, it is important enough that it affects the rest of the sculpture's message, as Sanborn stated in an article, "They didn't have everything to work with that I wanted them to have to work with."[6] As of Autumn 2009, the last part of the puzzle remains unsolved.

CHAPTER 4

Symbolism

V ⊲⊐∪⊡⊾⌐∨⊐

Steeling himself for the last step of his journey,
the initiate shifted his muscular frame and turned
his attention back to the skull cradled in his palms.
The crimson wine looked almost black in the dim
candlelight. The chamber had fallen deathly silent,
and he could feel all of the witnesses watching him,
waiting for him to take his final oath
and join their elite ranks. . . .

"May this wine I now drink become a deadly poison
to me . . . should I ever knowingly
or willfully violate my oath."
THE LOST SYMBOL, PAGE 5

About an hour's drive east of Lisbon, Portugal, lies the town of Evora.
In the Roman Empire, the town was an important military center
called Liberalitas Julia, and it was the headquarters of the commander Quintus Sertorius from 80 to 72 B.C. Near the center of the town
stands an impressive ruin of a Roman temple. Mistakenly pegged
today as the "Temple of Diana," it was more likely a temple dedicated to the supreme Roman god, Jove. Its surviving fourteen
Corinthian columns make an impressive tourist attraction today, in
spite of the temple's more grisly post-Roman past as a slaughterhouse
and an execution site during the Portuguese Inquisition. The violence
of the Spanish Inquisition is better known, but the Portuguese coun-
terpart lasted later than any other across Europe, up until the mid-
1770s. While the American Revolution was busy separating church
from state, the Catholic Church was still busy roasting the feet off

heretics in the Portuguese countryside. But I didn't come to Evora to look at a pile of crumbling Roman ruins. I traveled to this isolated town to see something a whole lot creepier.

At varying times after the Romans, Evora has been ruled by pagan Visigoths, Islamic Moors, and eventually Catholic kings by the twelfth century. For a while, it was the location of the court of the Kingdom of Portugal. A few blocks from the Temple of Diana stands the Igreja Real de São Francisco (Royal Church of St. Francis), where the kings of Portugal worshipped for centuries. This region of the country is known for its exquisite mosaics, and the church has breathtaking blue-and-white tile walls, surmounted by gilded wood and plasterwork. But these spectacular details hide a grim secret. Behind the main altar of the church is a small chapel. The visitor enters under an archway inscribed with the foreboding message, *Nós ossos que aqui estamos, pelos vossos esperamos*: "Our bones that are here wait for yours."

The Capela dos Ossos, or Chapel of Bones, is an architectural monument to the contemplation of death. In the sixteenth century, monks removed the bones of nearly 5,000 of their brethren from the

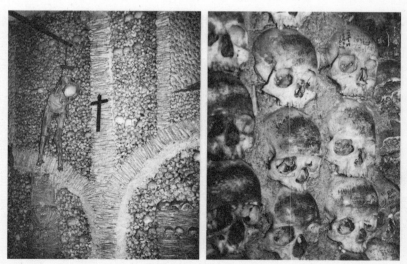

The walls, pillars, and ceilings of the Capela dos Ossos *in Evora, Portugal, are filled with the bones of 5,000 monks.*

town's more than forty monastic cemeteries and brought them to this place. The bones and skulls of the monks line almost every square inch of wall space, with stacks of tibias, fibulas, and femurs forming a macabre pattern everywhere you look. The term "ribbed vault" takes on new meaning here. Grinning, eyeless skulls peer out of the walls and archways, and the skeletal corpses of an adult and a baby hang on one side of the room. Latin phrases appear here and there: "The day that I die is better than the day I was born" and "I leave, but I will not die."

Memento Mori

The skull has appeared for centuries as a common symbol of mortality, not only in various degrees of Masonic ritual but in many other historical, fraternal, and religious organizations. The Latin term *memento mori* means "remember, you will die" and is often accompanied by a depiction of a skull as a reminder of the end of physical life.

Dan Brown's description of the ritual for the 33° of the Scottish Rite, quoted at the beginning of this chapter, is not accurate; such a ceremony does not take place in that degree, and his inspiration for the ceremony is discussed in Chapter 2. That's not to say, however, that skulls and other symbolism of death have never played a part in

A common nineteenth-century Masonic Knights Templar apron design. Collection of the author.

Masonic ritual. A line in the Fellow Craft degree of Masonic ritual informs the brother that the mason's tool, the level, reminds us that "we are traveling along the level of time, to that undiscover'd country, from whose bourn no traveler returns."[1] And the death of the architect of Solomon's Temple plays a central part in the Master Mason degree.

In addition, skulls and death imagery are more plentiful in some jurisdictions outside of the U.S.

Skulls have had a role in the Knights Templar order of the York Rite of Freemasonry. The skull and crossbones is a legendary symbol of the medieval order of warrior monks. For decades, the aprons worn by the Masonic Knights Templar in their meetings featured a skull and crossbones. The practice was ended in the 1920s, but the aprons are commonly found for sale on eBay.

Reminders of death and mortality are not solely Masonic symbols. Skulls have appeared in art for centuries. A famous first-century mosaic was found on a tabletop of the city of Pompeii that looks almost Masonic in its use of building tools combined with a skull. The grinning skull is balanced on a wheel of fortune, with a butterfly symbolizing the soul. The clothes and symbols of wealth and power are on the left, while poverty and the clothes of a beggar are on the right, with Death in the center as the great leveler.

A memento mori *image on a table discovered in the city of Pompeii.*

In the sixteenth and seventeenth centuries, a type of painting known as *vanitas* became popular in France, Flanders, and the Netherlands. A skull, rotting fruit, snuffed candles, hourglasses, and objects depicting transitory wealth on Earth were popular still-life subjects as a message to remind the viewer that "all is vanity" when compared to our ultimate, common end as a feast for worms. Such grim reminders were not considered macabre, especially at a time when life expectancy was way too short, infant mortality was shockingly high, medical care was more dumb luck than science, and Death was always hanging around the door to your hovel.

Drinking from a skull is hardly a Masonic innovation. Perhaps the most famous skull goblet in history belonged to George Gordon, Lord Byron, which he immortalized in his 1808 poem, *Lines Inscribed Upon a Cup Formed from a Skull*. It reads, in part:

> Start not nor deem my spirit fled;
> In me behold the only skull
> From which, unlike a living head,
> Whatever flows is never dull.
>
> I lived, I loved, I quaffed, like thee:
> I died: let earth my bones resign;
> Fill up—thou canst not injure me;
> The worm hath fouler lips than thine.
>
> Better to hold the sparkling grape,
> Than nurse the earth-worm's slimy brood;
> And circle in the goblet's shape
> The drink of gods, than reptile's food.
>
> Where once my wit, perchance, hath shone,
> In aid of others' let me shine;
> And when, alas! our brains are gone,
> What nobler substitute than wine?

The legend was that the young Byron ransacked the graves of his ancestors on the family estate, Newstead Abbey, and had a drinking cup made of one of their skulls. Byron himself told a slightly different version:

> The gardener in digging discovered a skull that had probably belonged to some jolly friar or monk of the Abbey about the time it was demonasteried. Observing it to be of giant size and in a perfect state of preservation, a strange fancy seized me of having it set and mounted as a drinking cup. I accordingly sent it to town, and it returned to me with a very high polish and of a mottled colour like tortoiseshell.[2]

The Hand of the Mysteries

In *The Lost Symbol*, Robert Langdon is brought to the U.S. Capitol building to give a lecture. Why this university professor hasn't developed a keen sense of skepticism and lie-detecting sixth sense after teaching college students is something of a puzzler. Nevertheless, Langdon believes he has been invited by his friend and mentor, Peter Solomon, the head of the Smithsonian Institute, and a 33° Free-mason. But upon arriving at the Capitol dome rotunda, a scream is heard from a tourist who has discovered a recently severed hand, stuck to a wooden base and still bleeding. Langdon eventually gets around to examining it and discovers a series of tattoos on the hand and fingers. He describes it as a real-life copy of the Hand of the Mysteries, "one of the most secretive icons of the ancient world."[3] It's only secretive from the standpoint that few people have heard of it before *The Lost Symbol*.

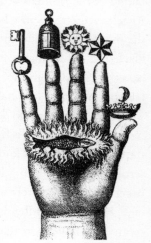

The Hand of the Philosophers with Its Secret Signs *by Johan Isaac Hollandus (1667).*

The thumb is tattooed with a crown, the index finger with a star, the middle finger with a sun, the ring finger with a lantern, and the little finger with a key. Langdon explains that the hand is a summons, an invitation to receive secret, protected wisdom "known only to an elite few."

Dan Brown has said in interviews that one of his favorite research books is Manly P. Hall's *The Secret Teachings of All Ages*, and if you were an author of thrillers with esoteric, mysterious and arcane plot points and imagery, it would be your favorite, too. This seems to be the source of his description of the Hand of the Mysteries.

Today, he is mostly unheard of except among those with an interest in very esoteric subjects, but between 1920 and the 1970s, Manly Palmer Hall was a superstar in the crowded world of psychics and occult scholars. A Canadian-born transplant to Los Angeles, Hall went from a teenager with a sixth-grade education to world-renowned author, teacher, and speaker in just ten short years. Hall wrote volumes of books and pamphlets on ancient mysteries, religions, and magical beliefs. He had radio and television shows and could pack the largest lecture and concert halls for his speeches. His "Big Book," *The Secret Teachings of All Ages*, published in 1928, was a massive undertaking of the printer's art, and catapulted Hall from just another Los Angeles storefront preacher to the world's most consulted expert on the metaphysical. It featured beautiful color illustrations, hundreds of black-and-white images from obscure sources around the world, and passages culled from more than 600 references. Weighing in at fourteen pounds in its original format, it cost an astonishing $100 (which would be more than $1,200 today). To date, it has sold more than a million copies, and it is by far the most popular book ever written on the world of esoteric knowledge.[4] Unfortunately, Hall wasn't always scrupulous about citing his sources, sometimes out of forgetfulness, other times deliberately so his facts couldn't be checked.

Hall coyly ascribes his explanation of the Hand of the Mysteries to an "unknown" artist and author. In fact, the original source is the seventeenth-century work, *The Hand of the Philosophers with Its Secret Signs*, by Johan Isaac Hollandus.[5] Hollandus describes the hand as being filled with secret signs that only those who took the oaths of the alchemists would be able to understand—then goes on to explain them anyway. Each symbol is of an important substance used in practical alchemy's chemical processes. The thumb's crown symbolizes saltpeter, the "King and Lord of all salts," which were vital in the chemical processes of alchemy. The forefinger's six-pointed star stands for vitriol, a caustic acid compound. The middle finger's sun represents *sal ammoniacum*, or salts of ammonia. The ring finger's lantern represents alum. The little finger's key, representing common salt, is the Key of the Philosophers that unlocks the rest of the hand. Not mentioned by Dan Brown in *The Lost Symbol* is the middle of the hand, which contains a fish surrounded by fire. The fish represents mercury,

for without Mercury, or the fish, nothing can be done. He is
the beginning, the middle and the end, and he is the priest who
must marry everything. And he is the male and the seed; he is
the water out of which all metals have originated; and he is the
principal (factor) of all Arts, and the greatest of all secrets.[6]

The seventh sign is the fire in the palm surrounding the fish, signifying sulfur.

It is the earth and beginning of all metals. It is the female who
brings forth the fruit. For no seed can grow unless it be first
thrown into fertile soil. Then beautiful fruit will come from it.
Thus it also happens that when a pure Mercury is joined to a
pure Sulphur, it brings forth pure fruit. Thus, they are man and
woman, father and mother, fire and water, seed and earth.[7]

What follows Hollandus's explanation of the secret elements that
make up each finger are chemical processes that describe each step in
code by saying "add the third finger," and so on. If you were to read
the recipes and didn't know what chemical each finger stood for, you
would be stumped. Hollandus's explanation is purely practical, so
Manly P. Hall provided the philosophical meat to the story.

[T]he figure symbolizes the hand of a Master Mason with
which he "raises" the martyred Builder of the Divine House.
Philosophically the key represents the Mysteries themselves,
without whose aid man cannot unlock the numerous chambers
of his own being. The lantern is human knowledge, for it is a
spark of the Universal Fire captured in a man-made vessel; it is
the light of those who dwell in the inferior universe and with the
aid of which they seek to follow in the footsteps of Truth. The
sun, which may be termed the " light of the world," represents
the luminescence of creation through which man may learn the
mystery of all creatures which express through form and number. The star is the Universal Light which reveals cosmic and
celestial verities. The crown is Absolute Light—unknown and
unrevealed—whose power shines through all the lesser lights

that are but sparks of this Eternal Effulgence. Thus is set forth the right hand, or active principle, of Deity, whose works are all contained within the "hollow of His hand."[8]

The Circumpunct

[There is] represented in every regular and well-governed lodge a certain " point within a circle . . ."[9]

The director Alfred Hitchcock is generally credited with the origin of the word "MacGuffin." He used it to describe the central idea of a movie plot that propels the story forward. It might be the search for a lost pearl necklace, buried treasure, plans for a secret weapon, the Holy Grail, or a missing cousin. It usually doesn't matter exactly what the MacGuffin is, because you should be really interested in the characters and whether they survive in the end.

The Lost Symbol has as its propelling MacGuffin a "lost symbol" that Mal'akh is hunting. Near the book's climax, Mal'akh forces Peter Solomon to reveal the "lost symbol" that the Freemasons have protected for centuries. He lies to Mal'akh and tells him it is the *circumpunct*: (•)

It's likely, because of the influence of Brown's book on popular culture, that this odd term will quickly become the *de facto* name of this very ancient symbol, even though most who have encountered the symbol—a point within a circle—in literature, symbolism, and archeology have never heard it called that.

The point within a circle is one of the oldest symbols on Earth. It is the alchemical sign for gold, the element said to have come from the gods. It was the symbol of the notorious Bavarian Illuminati (1776–1791) and was said to represent an open eye. The Chippewa Indians used the symbol to depict the Spirit. In the mystical Jewish belief system Kabbalah, the symbol is called Kether, ‏כתר‎, which means "crown" and is the first Sephirah of the Tree of Life, the highest on its middle pillar.

But its principal use over the centuries has been to depict the sun. It appears in Egyptian hieroglyphics as "Ra" (sun), and it is common in astrological texts, as well. The point generally indicates the sun itself, while the circle depicts the universe. The circle is a shape with no beginning and no end—a fitting illustration of an infinite concept.

In modern times, it is also a simple representation of hydrogen, showing one proton and one electron—interesting, since hydrogen is the primary element that makes up the sun, and with a bit of a stretch, could provide admittedly tenuous link to the explosion of Katherine Solomon's lab in *The Lost Symbol* from its hydrogen power plant.

A point within a circle, with vertical lines representing Saint John the Baptist and Saint John the Evangelist, as depicted in Freemasonry. From an early twentieth century glass slide.

The circumpunct does appear in Freemasonry, even though most Masons would never know it by that name. A description of its role in the ritual ceremony of the Entered Apprentice shows some modifications in both design and explanation from the classic representation of a point within a circle.

> [There is] represented in every regular and well-governed lodge a certain "point within a circle," the point representing an individual brother, the circle the boundary-line of his conduct beyond which he is never to suffer his prejudices or passions to betray him. This circle is embodied by two perpendicular parallel lines, representing St. John the Baptist and St. John the Evangelist; and upon the top rest the Holy Scriptures. In going around this circle, we necessarily touch upon these two lines, as well as upon the Holy Scriptures; and while a Mason keeps himself circumscribed within their precepts it is impossible that he should materially err.[10]

The Masonic version of the symbol is actually based on an astrological version, with some modifications. In this variation, the point in the center represents the Earth, which in medieval times was thought to be the center of the universe. The heavens were believed to spin around the Earth, represented by the circle. The two lines represented the summer and winter solstices (Cancer and Capricorn), the longest and shortest days of the year. For thousands of years, these days were celebrated as pagan feast days all over the world, and they were especially important to farming societies, because the solstices served astronomical markers for determining planting seasons.

As with many Masonic traditions, the connection of the solstices to Freemasonry runs through the Catholic Church. Even though Freemasonry today is nondenominational and nonsectarian, most rituals found in Masonic lodges in the United States state that Masons come "from the Holy Saints John of Jerusalem." In about 300 A.D., the Catholic Church began dedicating popular pagan feast days to the saints. June 21, the longest day of the year, was declared Saint John the Baptist day, while December 22, the shortest day, was dedicated to Saint John the Evangelist. With drifting calendars over the centuries, the more modern dates have shifted to June 24 and December 27.

Freemasonry was first developed when Roman Catholicism was the prevailing religion, and these feast days continued under the Church of England. It was common for guilds and other trade groups to adopt patron saints. The Masons eventually picked both Saint John the Baptist and Saint John the Evangelist (collectively, Masons refer to them as the Holy Saints John), and Freemasons celebrate their feast days with banquets, called festive boards or table lodges. In fact, the formation of the first Grand Lodge of Freemasons in London in June 1717 was motivated out of a desire to revive the custom of an annual feast on St. John the Evangelist day.

There is another explanation for why these two saints were picked by the Masons and added to a simple symbol that was used to explain a Freemason's outward and inward conduct. John the Baptist was zealous, while John the Evangelist was more learned and philosophical, so by picking both of them as patron saints, Masons symbolically balanced passion and reason. The symbol also shows the Bible, or Volume of Sacred Law, at the top of the circle. In Freemasonry, the point represents the individual, not the sun, and the circle is the boundary of his actions. Taken as a whole, the symbol teaches that a Mason should consult the Bible, or the sacred texts of his own religion, to realize the proper balance between passion and intensity on one side, and knowledge and education on the other. In other words, he should balance education, enthusiasm, and faith equally to effectively subdue his passions.

The symbolism in Masonry extends further. To draw a perfect circle, you need to use a compass, which is one of the two primary symbolic tools of Freemasonry (it appears paired with the square in the most commonly seen "logo" of the fraternity). In Masonic ritual, the purpose of the compass is to circumscribe the Mason's passions and desires and to keep him "within due bounds" with all of society. The symbol of the point within the circle and two parallel lines illustrates this same idea.

Dan Brown did not invent the term circumpunct, even though it is a very new name for a very old symbol. Even the up-to-date, online version of the venerable *Oxford English Dictionary* has no definition of the term; at least it didn't before *The Lost Symbol* came along. As a word, it certainly would be the proper Latin way of describing such a symbol, but while "point within a circle" seems like a clumsy, nontechnical, nonspiritual way to describe a simple pictogram for literally thousands of years, that seems to be the reality. Obviously, Dan Brown wrestled with this as well and settled on the obscure term *circumpunct*. It seems to have been coined no earlier than 1992 by followers of "Brian the Cyber-prophet," the creator of "Brianism," a 1990s spoof of religion.[11]

Given the end of Brown's story and the subsequent explanation by Peter Solomon of the "lost symbol," consider one other interesting appearance of the circumpunct. In aerial photographs of the Washington Monument on the Mall in Washington, D.C., the obelisk of the monument, which is said to represent a shaft of sunlight reaching up to the sun, or to God, stands in the center of a broad circular walkway, surrounded by flagpoles. From straight above, it looks remarkably like a point within a circle.

Ouroboros

In *The Lost Symbol*, Mal'akh has the symbol of the *Serpens Candivorens*, a snake coiled in a circle swallowing its own tail, tattooed around the crown of his head. The symbol, called the *ouroboros* by the Greeks, represents the infinite cycle of nature's endless creation and destruction—life and death. The image is a common one and was popular in

An ouroboros.

the seventeenth and eighteenth centuries in published esoteric works, sometimes accompanied by the saying: "All is one." Dan Brown explains it as the origin of the word atonement: *at one ment.*

The image first appears in Egyptian religious symbolism as a depiction of the sun's constant daily and yearly cycle. In Greek literature, Plato's Socratic dialogue *Timaeus*, written in 368 B.C., describes such a circular beast as the first creature created in the universe, which became the Earth itself:

> Now the creation took up the whole of each of the four elements; for the Creator compounded the world out of all the fire and all the water and all the air and all the earth, leaving no part of any of them nor any power of them outside. . . .
>
> For the Creator conceived that a being which was self-sufficient would be far more excellent than one which lacked anything; and, as he had no need to take anything or defend himself against any one, the Creator did not think it necessary to bestow upon him hands: nor had he any need of feet, nor of the

whole apparatus of walking; but the movement suited to his spherical form was assigned to him, being of all the seven that which is most appropriate to mind and intelligence; and he was made to move in the same manner and on the same spot, within his own limits revolving in a circle. All the other six motions were taken away from him, and he was made not to partake of their deviations. And as this circular movement required no feet, the universe was created without legs and without feet.

Such was the whole plan of the eternal God about the god that was to be, to whom for this reason he gave a body, smooth and even, having a surface in every direction equidistant from the centre, a body entire and perfect, and formed out of perfect bodies. And in the centre he put the soul, which he diffused throughout the body, making it also to be the exterior environment of it; and he made the universe a circle moving in a circle, one and solitary, yet by reason of its excellence able to converse with itself, and needing no other friendship or acquaintance. Having these purposes in view he created the world a blessed god.[12]

In Gnosticism, the image was related to the solar god Abraxas and signified eternity and the soul of the world. In alchemy, it represented the spirit of Mercury, a substance that was believed to permeate all matter and symbolized continuous renewal. Because a snake sheds its skin and appears to have been reborn, it has often appeared as a symbol of resurrection and the cycle of life and death. In alchemy, a double ouroboros (two creatures swallowing one another, in the shape of a figure eight) signifies volatility.

A snake appeared in the early Scottish Rite's 25° ceremony, "Knight of the Brazen Serpent." Originally, this degree told the story related in the biblical account of the Israelites in their fortieth year of wandering in the desert. Without bread and water, they turned against Moses:

And the LORD sent fiery serpents among the people, and they bit the people; and much people of Israel died. / Therefore the people came to Moses, and said, We have sinned, for we have spoken against the LORD, and against thee; pray unto the LORD, that he take away the serpents from us. And Moses prayed for the people. / And the LORD said unto Moses, Make thee a fiery serpent, and set it upon a pole: and it shall come to pass, that every one that is bitten, when he looketh upon it, shall live. / And Moses made a serpent of brass, and put it upon a pole, and it came to pass, that if a serpent had bitten any man, when he beheld the serpent of brass, he lived.

Numbers 21:6–9

This story may be the origin of the medical symbol of a single snake entwined around a pole. In any case, the 25° of the Scottish Rite has been rewritten over the years in the United States, and the stories told in the Northern and Southern Jurisdictions are completely different. In fact, while the 25° is still called "Knight of the Brazen Serpent" in the Southern Jurisdiction, in the North it has been moved to the 6°, where the Moses story is still told.

Jachin, Boaz, and the Winding Staircase

As Mal'akh stands in front of a mirror admiring his tattoos and muttering, "I am a masterpiece," he describes his legs being inked with images of two architectural columns. These are Jachin and Boaz, the two brass (or bronze) pillars that stood outside the porch of King Solomon's Temple, as described in the Bible.

And king Solomon sent and fetched Hiram out of Tyre. / He was a widow's son of the tribe of Naphtali, and his father was a man of Tyre, a worker in brass: and he was filled with wisdom, and understanding, and cunning to work all works in brass. And he came to king Solomon, and wrought all his work. / For he cast two pillars of brass, of eighteen cubits high apiece: and a line of twelve cubits did compass either of them about. . . .

And he set up the pillars in the porch of the temple: and he set up the right pillar, and called the name thereof Jachin: and he set up the left pillar, and called the name thereof Boaz. / And upon the top of the pillars was lily work: so was the work of the pillars finished.

I Kings 7:13–22[13]

Jachin is believed to mean "he establishes," while Boaz means "in him is strength." While two substantial pillars standing on either side of a doorway are popular architectural features, and have been for centuries, representations specifically of Jachin and Boaz are not uncommon. They symbolize strength and establishment, and in the modern world, they frequently appear on the entries of libraries, courthouses, government buildings, banks, and school buildings. They are supposed to represent the wisdom and justice of King Solomon.

Jachin and Boaz, and the Winding Staircase. From an early twentieth-century glass slide.

The ultimate fate of the columns is referred to in the Bible in Jeremiah 52:17:

Also the pillars of brass that were in the house of the LORD, and the bases, and the brasen sea that was in the house of the LORD, the Chaldeans brake, and carried all the brass of them to Babylon.

To Freemasons, these columns are a vital element within the lodge room itself and within Masonic ritual. In the United States especially, representations of Jachin and Boaz are dominating pieces of architectural sculpture, and they are the gateway to a portion of the Fellow Craft degree in most ceremonies used in America, called the "Middle Chamber." In this extended lecture, the Mason is symbolically led into the Middle Chamber of King Solomon's Temple to receive his education, and then his "wages" as a new Fellow Craft. The lecture explains the five classical orders of architecture, as set down by the first-century B.C. Roman architect Marcus Polio Vitruvius (Tuscan, Ionic, Doric, Corinthian, and Composite). The Fellow Craft is led up a flight of winding stairs, and each step represents a different portion of the liberal arts and sciences, and each of the five senses. In short, it is a crash course in a liberal arts education. The winding staircase itself is a symbol of the twisting path of education to enlightenment, with each turn ahead obscured from view.

All of this probably sounds quaint to the modern mind, where such topics are covered in basic grade school education. But the Fellow Craft degree and the Middle Chamber lecture is a connection with an earlier time, when the average citizen was not well educated and public schools did not yet exist. The Masonic lodge may well have been the first time a man encountered these ideas in the eighteenth century, and the ceremony was designed to acquaint him with these new and unusual concepts of grammar, logic, rhetoric, geometry, arithmetic, music, and astronomy. The goal of the lodge is to improve mankind by improving men, and education is the most important achievement.

In *The Lost Symbol*, the winding staircase appears in several locations:

- Mal'akh has a winding staircase tattooed on his back, rising up his spine to the base of his brain. He sees it as a symbol of the rising steps of knowledge to true intellectual and spiritual enlightenment, and eventually, his transformation to a higher being.
- In the Capitol, the winding staircases into the basement conceal Peter Solomon's private Chamber of Reflection.
- The stone pyramid's riddles eventually show a winding staircase beneath Heredom, a mythical mountain sacred to the Scottish Rite, and Robert Langdon believes, mistakenly, that it leads to the basement of the Scottish Rite's House of the Temple.
- In the end, Peter Solomon reveals that the winding staircase of the Washington Monument leads down to the location of the Lost Word, the cornerstone where the Bible was buried.

Pyramids

Most people agree that the unfinished pyramid on the reverse side of the Great Seal of the United States, as seen on the back of the dollar bill, is a Masonic symbol. In the opening sequence of the 2005 film *National Treasure*, Christopher Plummer, playing kindly old treasure hunter Grandpa Gates, tells his grandson that the Freemasons put it on the dollar. Unfortunately, it isn't true, though there are elements of the seal that share a connection to Masonic symbols. In 1884, Harvard Professor Charles Eliot Norton wrote that the unfinished pyramid and the All-Seeing Eye on the reverse of the Great Seal of the United States "can hardly, (however artistically treated by the designer), look otherwise than as a dull emblem of a Masonic fraternity." This is most probably the source of the mistaken belief that it is a Masonic symbol.[14]

Pyramids do not play a role in Masonic symbolism found in the degrees of the Masonic lodge, the York Rite, or the Scottish Rite. They don't even pop up in the Middle Eastern-themed degree of the Shriners. Pyramids, finished or unfinished, are not Masonic symbols.

Dan Brown's storyline in *The Lost Symbol* involving a secret stone pyramid, with a gold capstone, is pure fiction. Masons don't revere pyramids, worship them, or carry them around in lumpy backpacks when they visit Washington, D.C.

It's true that there are Egyptian-themed Masonic lodge rooms and buildings, but the reason has little to do with secret symbols. A notable example is Naval Lodge No. 4 in Washington, D.C., a few blocks from the Capitol on Pennsylvania Avenue. Its lodge room is decorated in an Egyptian motif because its members

The Egyptian-themed lodge room of Washington's Naval Lodge No. 4.

helped to drag the original cornerstone of the Egyptian-inspired Washington Monument from the city's dock to its worksite.

Egyptian-influenced architecture became popular in the 1800s, just as classical Greek styles had in the 1700s. Interest grew when news came to Europe of the discovery of Queen Hatshepsut's temple and the mummies of pharaohs at Deir el Bahri. Egyptmania returned again in the 1920s, when Howard Carter discovered the tomb of King Tutankhamen and its dazzling artifacts. It was the major inspiration behind Art Deco architecture, art, and design in the 1930s. Suddenly, everything from banks and gas stations to post offices and movie theaters was laden with Egyptian-inspired Art Deco details. The Freemasons got into the act with Philadelphia's Grand Lodge building, Detroit's Masonic Temple, Indiana Freemasons' Hall and dozens more. But aside from these architectural embellishments, there is no Egyptian symbolism in regular, recognized Freemasonry as practiced in the United States.

Nevertheless, there are a handful of tenuous connections between Egyptian mythology and Masonic practices.

In 1713, a French Abbot named Jean Terrasson published a three-volume romantic novel called *Sethos* about ancient Egypt. His trilogy tells of a prince who undergoes three trials, is initiated into the mysterious worship of the Egyptian goddess Isis, and is taught the ideals of brotherhood, truth, justice, and knowledge—all of which sounds very similar to Freemasonry. Lots of Masons fell in love with the notion of the Mystery Schools of Egypt, as Terrasson had described them. In fact, in his *Constitutions* of 1723, the first modern document of speculative Freemasonry, Reverend James Anderson asserted that the Hebrew Abraham taught the Egyptians the seven liberal arts and sciences and that the Alexandrian mathematician Euclid taught the Egyptian nobility the art of geometry in the third century B.C.

Karl Friedrich von Koppen (1734–1797) founded a little-known order of the *Afrikanische Bauherren* (African Architects) in 1767. Its degrees claimed the first Grand Master of Freemasonry was the biblical character of Ham, who went to Egypt and took the name Menes. There he supposedly received secret knowledge that was passed down through the centuries, eventually to Herr Koppen. It seems to have vanished pretty quickly.

An Egyptian Rite was founded in Naples, Italy, in 1777, and its most famous purveyor was Giuseppe Balsamo (1743–1795), better known to history as Count Alessandro di Cagliostro. A notorious character in the years just before the French Revolution, Cagliostro claimed to have lived for 2,000 years. A self-styled magician, he told the tale that he had been initiated into the Egyptian Rite at the base of the Great Pyramid in Giza. He died imprisoned in Italy's Fortress of San Leo after being sentenced to death (reduced to a life sentence by the pope) by the Inquisition for being a Freemason.[15]

In 1789, Ignaz von Born, a member of a lodge in Vienna, Austria, published an essay comparing Masonic ritual to Egyptian ceremonies. Never mind that no one really knew exactly what those Egyptian ceremonies were. A combination of the novel *Sethos* and von Born's essays, along with some German fairy tales and some Masonic themes, influenced his lodge brother Wolfgang Amadeus Mozart's opera *The Magic Flute*. Yet, most Masons today who watch or listen to The Magic Flute recognize almost nothing having to do with the Freemasonry they know.

In the 1800s, two Egyptian-influenced Masonic-style degree systems—the Rite of Memphis and the Rite of Mizraim—were created in France, largely as moneymaking schemes for their promoters. Both rites had more than ninety different degrees, and in both cases, they were peddled mostly as enterprises selling lavish diplomas with high-sounding titles for ready cash. The more ancient, exotic, and mysterious the rituals seemed, the more they were lapped up by excited initiates, and it was hard to get more ancient and exotic than the land of the pharaohs. These rites were shut down by the government of France as well as by the country's largest Grand Lodge, the Grand Orient of France, but they never totally died out until their inventors and hucksters passed on. In recent years, these rituals have been dug up and have reemerged on the Internet, but they are not a part of the accepted Masonic world.

The All-Seeing Eye

Most people have probably seen the letter *G* depicted in the center of the Masonic square and compass. The *G* is the initial of both geometry and God, or the Grand Architect of the Universe (a phrase used in Masonic ritual to describe God). Early stonemasons believed that the sacred science of geometry, which seemed so mysterious to the masses, must have been given to the masons of the Bible's great building projects by God himself. Like the cathedrals built by the operative stonemason

guilds, modern Freemasonry unites the concepts of God and geometry, fusing faith with science. In most North American lodges, the *G* appears over the Master's chair and is generally illuminated when the lodge is open. But in lodges in non-English speaking countries, the words for geometry and God frequently do not begin with *G*, and in countries that use a completely different alphabet, the letter *G* may not exist at all.

George Washington's Masonic embroidered apron, featuring the All-Seeing Eye. Given to Washington by Marquis de Lafayette in August 1784. It is now on display in the museum of the Grand Lodge of Pennsylvania.

Therefore, the "All-Seeing Eye" is used to represent God, and it frequently appears inside an illuminated equilateral triangle. The triangle represents the mathematical perfection of geometry, although its origins as a Christian symbol for God can be traced back for centuries, with the three sides representing the Christian trinity. It is by no means a uniquely Masonic symbol.

The first appearance of the All-Seeing Eye as a published Masonic symbol used in ritual ceremonies of the time seems to be in Thomas Smith Webb's *Freemasons' Monitor*, published in 1797. However, the All-Seeing Eye does appear on hand-painted or hand-embroidered Masonic aprons earlier than this, including an apron reputedly given to George Washington by Lafayette in August 1784.

The Perfect Ashlar

In *The Lost Symbol*, Robert Langdon and Katherine Solomon meet Father Galloway at the National Cathedral, where they discuss the stone pyramid and another stone block that belonged to Peter Solomon. Galloway refers to the smooth cube as the perfect ashlar.

In a Masonic lodge, there are two stones to be found, one rough, the other smooth. They are called the rough and perfect ashlars, and the origin is from the stonemasons art. The rough ashlar is a rude and imperfect chunk of rock as it is removed from the quarry. It holds the

potential to become part of a building or a piece of sculpture, or it could be rejected and tossed on the heap of discarded stone. The perfect ashlar is a similar stone that has been squared and dressed with smooth sides, ready to become part of a beautiful structure. Obviously, the two stones are metaphors for character building.

Masonic jewelry in the United States and Canada has always been popular, but in Europe where Masonophobia has always been more common, members rarely display symbols of their allegiance. That didn't stop them from being more clever about it. A common item for Masons was a watch fob, a bauble that was attached to a man's pocket watch chain. On the outside, it resembled a gold ball or cube. Unlocked, unhinged, and opened, it revealed a cruciform-shaped piece, made up of pyramid-shaped seg-

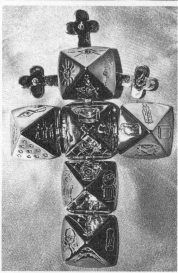

"The Perfect Ashlar" watch fob—closed, and opened to reveal its hidden symbols and cruciform shape.

71

ments, and each side was engraved with a different Masonic symbol. The gold ball version of this type of fob was called an orb. The square version is called *the perfect ashlar*.

Dan Brown describes the stone box of the small pyramid's capstone in *The Lost Symbol* as opening up into this very kind of cruciform shape.

Chamber of Reflection

In *The Lost Symbol*, Robert Langdon and a search party discover a Chamber of Reflection hidden in the bowels of the U.S. Capitol building. Since hardly anyone in that building engages in much mental reflection these days, it should not be surprising to find that Brown has taken liberties with the location. In reality, Masons don't place these rooms in public places, job sites, or even their home.

The use of a Chamber of Reflection is by no means a common practice in the United States, and most American Masons would give you a blank stare if you asked them about it. Freemasonry has different customs and practices around the world, and many jurisdictions outside of the United States do place their new candidates in such a gloomy place prior to their initiation. The purpose is to compel the candidate to examine his motives for joining the fraternity and contemplate his own mortality—and perhaps to scare the bejeebers out of those who aren't taking the experience seriously. The candidate is usually asked to write his last will and testament, which cannot help but place a little spark of worry in his head that he may not survive the evening.

In some jurisdictions, upon exiting the Chamber of Reflection, a brother dressed in a black-hooded Death costume confronts the candidate and asks questions to make certain he is not seeking membership out of mere curiosity. Again, this is by no means a universal practice, and it is almost unheard of in the United States.

On the table before him in the chamber are a lit candle, a skull and crossed tibiae (leg bones), an hourglass, bread and water, small bowls of sulfur and salt, a pen, and a piece of paper. In some chambers, there is also an image of a rooster, and the word *vitriol* appears.

The items in the Chamber of Reflection have been drawn from images in alchemical rites. The skull and bones are the universal symbols of mortality, as discussed earlier in this chapter. The hourglass tells the candidate that time is short. The bread and water are symbols of simplicity. The sulfur, salt, and vitriol are chemicals used in alchemy, and the rooster is a symbol of Hermes, or Mercury, who crows at the dawning of the day announcing the coming of light.

The chamber itself is usually painted black or textured to look like the interior of a cave. This is to symbolize the inner aspects of the conscience, as well as to recall the sort of caves religious hermits retired to in order to separate themselves form the outer world and focus their contemplation.

Dan Brown refers to the term *vitriol* as something of a Masonic mantra. This is not really the case. It is an alchemical term, and is in fact an acronym. V:.I:.T:.R:.I:.O:.L:. stands for the Latin phrase, *Visita Interiora Terrae Rectificando Invenies Occultum Lapidem*, which means "Visit the interior of the Earth, and by rectifying, you shall find the hidden stone." Alchemy searched for the "Philosopher's Stone," the elixir that would change base metals to gold. But the Masonic use of the term *vitriol* urges the candidate to examine his own life, and by working to improve himself, he will find his own "philosopher's stone" that will change his base character into gold. It's a more erudite way of expressing, "Know thyself."

CHAPTER 5

The Scottish Rite

>⊓◻ ∨ᴸᴇ>>ᴦ∨⊓ ᴦᴦ>◻

I'm the president of the shadow government
The grand governor of the federal reserve
Public enemy of the society
The one you cannot see
The 33 degree

"33 DEGREE" LYRICS, THIEVERY CORPORATION

The Ancient Accepted Scottish Rite of Freemasonry is perhaps the least understood and most maligned piece of the Masonic puzzle. It is first tied to Dan Brown's *The Lost Symbol* by the central symbol depicted on the cover of the first U.S. hardback edition: namely, the double-headed eagle, combined with the number *33*.

The Lost Symbol starts by describing a conferral of the 33° of the Scottish Rite on the book's villain, Mal'akh, and the ceremony is presented in a creepy (and incorrect) manner. Ritualistic terms, clothing, and paraphernalia are portrayed, and for anyone who has never been through initiation into a fraternity, sorority, or other similarly styled organization, the whole thing can seem frightening or silly, depending on your point of view.

Almost since the formation in this country of the Scottish Rite in the early 1800s, there has been a great misconception of the Rite's 32° and 33° within the structure of Freemasonry. Most non-Masons believe that, because the numbers are higher, the degrees are more advanced, and therefore, more important than the degrees taken in the local neighborhood Masonic lodge. As the lyrics of the band Thievery Corporation's song "33 Degree" suggest, these Masons in particular are believed by many conspiracy theorists to be the secret controlling force at work behind the New World Order and other nefarious (and in most cases nonexistent) organizations. In fact, *The Lost Symbol*'s Mal'akh seems to suffer from this same misconception, believing that attaining the 33° will give him access to the greatest secrets of the Freemasons.

The Ancient and Accepted Scottish Rite is a system of Freemasonry. In the United States, it is an appendant Masonic organization that offers additional degree experiences to 3° Master Masons. Despite its name, you don't have to be Scottish or go to Scotland to join, and it really isn't Scottish at all—its degrees and practices are primarily French. The name is believed to have come from the influence of Scottish Jacobite Masons living in exile in France in the early 1700s.

Of the 1.5 million Freemasons in the United States, approximately 500,000 are members of the Scottish Rite. The Rite confers its 4th through 32nd degrees on men who have already received their Master Mason degree (that is, the 3°) in their local lodge. The degrees teach further moral lessons, some of which continue the story of the building of King Solomon's Temple. Many have likened the Rite to "continuing education."

More than once I have had arguments with anti-Masons that have ended with the amusing accusation, "You don't know what you're talking about. I'll bet you haven't gone higher than the 15°!" The belief that 32° members of the Scottish Rite are somehow of higher rank or more exalted than a 3° Master Mason is false, as is the notion that only a certain rarified group attains the 32°, making them so-called high-ranking Freemasons. To become a 32° Scottish Rite Mason in the United States, it is not necessary to witness or participate in all twenty-nine of the Rite's degrees.

Because the degrees are presented as major theatrical productions that require large casts, props, scenery, lighting and music, not all of them are presented at one time for every class of candidates. Instead, they might simply receive a brief lecture or explanation of a degree and then be shown its signs and passwords; this is called "communicating" the degree. Many Scottish Rite chapters (called *valleys*) rotate the presentation of the other degrees over a period of years so a candidate can eventually see all of them. A candidate might participate in, for instance, the 4th, 14th, 18th, 30th, 31st and 32nd degrees, but not the others in between. As long as he has had the 32° conferred upon him, a man is considered a 32° Scottish Rite Mason. Outside of the United States, it may take many years to slowly advance through the degrees, but in the United States, joining the Scottish Rite almost assuredly makes you a 32° Mason.

Besides the twenty-nine degrees conferred on its members, the Scottish Rite also awards a 33° to a small percentage of members who have distinguished themselves or performed great services to the fraternity. There are approximately 11,000 men in the United States who are 33° Masons, and these are nonvoting, honorary positions. The governing board, known as the Supreme Council, is also made up of 33° members, known as "actives." Their authority only extends to the business of the Scottish Rite, and they have no say-so over any other Masonic organizations, including the state grand lodges—not exactly an all-powerful "inner circle." In fact, the Scottish Rite, like the other appendant organizations in the United States, operates in a each state or jurisdiction by agreeing not to step on the toes of that state's Grand Lodge or Grand Master. In the delicate dance of Masonic authority, the Scottish Rite is largely left alone to function as an independent body within the family of Freemasonry as long as its chapters promise not to confer the first three lodge degrees on new candidates.

North and South

There is no single international governing body of the Scottish Rite. Instead, in each country, it is governed by a Supreme Council, which is sovereign in its own jurisdiction. The United States is divided into two governing Scottish Rite bodies.

The Supreme Council of the Ancient and Accepted Scottish Rite, Southern Jurisdiction (SJ) was first formed in Charleston, South Carolina, in 1801; since 1870, it has been headquartered in Washington, D.C., in a building is known as the House of the Temple, located at 1733 16th Street NW. The Southern Jurisdiction governs the thirty-five states south of the Mason-Dixon Line and west of the Mississippi.

The Supreme Council of Ancient Accepted Scottish Rite of the Northern Masonic Jurisdiction (NMJ) governs the Rite in fifteen states, roughly north of the Mason-Dixon line and east of the Mississippi. It is headquartered in Lexington, Massachusetts. The Northern Jurisdiction, which was actually created by the Southern Jurisdiction between 1813 and 1815, has had a stormier history.

The Northern Masonic Jurisdiction dealt with competing, unauthorized Masonic organizations for many years, the most troublesome being headed by Joseph Cerneau, who was accused for years of peddling Masonic degrees far and wide for his own profit. "Cerneauism" became such a notorious problem in the Northeast United States that to this day, Freemasons visiting Pennsylvania Masonic lodges must take an oath that they are not members of a Cerneau lodge, even though Cerneau's competing Masonic and Scottish Rite system was generally shut down in 1867. Completely stamping out Cerneauism across the United States would take until the early 1900s.

Masonic author S. Brent Morris has said of the schism, "Confusing Cerneauism with regular Scottish Rite Masonry is like confusing the Church of Christ with the Church of Christ, Scientist. Their names are alike and their orders of worship are superficially similar, but they are fundamentally different denominations."[1]

Cerneauism nevertheless crept into Dan Brown's *The Lost Symbol*. The "drinking from a skull" sequence in the prologue of the novel is pulled from Joseph Cerneau's 33° ritual ceremony. It was published in 1887 as *Scotch Rite Masonry Illustrated* by the Reverend John Blanchard as an anti-Masonic exposé and was not an accurate portrayal of the 33° in the North or the South.

The Scottish Rite was one of the fastest-growing fraternal organizations in the late nineteenth century, largely due to the work of Albert Pike, who joined the Southern Jurisdiction in 1853. Pike was a self-made man of astonishing intellect—a lawyer, poet, editor, and student of ancient cultures, languages, philosophies, and religions. He believed that the degrees of the Scottish Rite held great potential for communicating important concepts, but he felt that the existing versions had lost much of their symbolic meaning. Taking it upon himself to rewrite the degrees, Pike added many layers of symbolism and allegory drawn from his wealth of knowledge. He designed the degrees to be presented in a dramatic setting, with a heavy dose of pageantry, which he felt would make a deeper and more lasting impression on candidates.

The Degrees of the Scottish Rite

All is revealed at the thirty-third degree . . .

The Lost Symbol, page 326

It is almost impossible to provide a superficial description of the degrees of the Scottish Rite. They have developed over 250 years or more of invention, rewrites, and knock-down, drag-out fights by competing scholars and jurisdictions.

The earliest degrees that would go on to become the basis of the Scottish Rite first appeared in the United States in 1767 and were brought to New York from France by a Dutch Mason named Henry Andrew Franken. Franken worked with another Frenchman, Etienne Morin, a trader in the West Indies, who possessed documents that authorized him to form new "high degree" bodies brought from Europe. In the 1770s, Franken crafted an English language version of the rituals, referred to now as the Franken Manuscript, and by 1786, he had degrees 4 through 25 completed. Additional degrees would follow until the creation of the Supreme Council in Charleston. Over the years, the Southern Jurisdiction has largely endeavored to keep Pike's versions of the degrees relatively intact. Some changes have been made to simplify Pike's sometimes labored Victorian language and pompous pageantry, but they remain, by and large, his vision of the degrees, mostly based on Old and New Testament sources, along with Pike's own references to other cultures and religions, and a sprinkling of alchemy and Kabbalah.

The Northern Masonic Jurisdiction set upon a different course, especially after about 1900, of altering their degrees on a regular basis, adding new ones, subtracting or moving old ones, and illustrating time-honored moral lessons with newer stories. As a result, instead of the degrees being largely Biblical in nature, degrees have been added over the years that tell patriotic stories or present morality tales with famous figures in more recent history. George Washington, Benedict Arnold, Benjamin Franklin, non-Mason Abraham Lincoln, and even Harry S Truman have appeared at various times in the NMJ's degree plays.

Nevertheless, it is useful to at least present the names of the current degrees of both systems.

SCOTTISH RITE DEGREES IN THE UNITED STATES

	Southern Jurisdiction	Northern Masonic Jurisdiction[2]
4°	Secret Master	Master Traveler
5°	Perfect Master	Perfect Master
6°	Intimate Secretary	Master of the Brazen Serpent
7°	Provost & Judge	Provost & Judge
8°	Intendant of the Building	Intendant of the Building
9°	Elu of the Nine	Master of the Temple
10°	Elu of the Fifteen	Master Elect
11°	Elu of the Twelve	Sublime Master Elected
12°	Master Architect	Grand Master Architect
13°	Royal Arch of Solomon	Master of the Ninth Arch
14°	Perfect Elu	Grand Elect Mason
15°	Knight of the East, or Knight of the Sword, or Knight of the Eagle	Knight of the East, or Knight of the Sword
16°	Prince of Jerusalem	Prince of Jerusalem
17°	Knight of the East and West	Knight of the East and West
18°	Knight Rose Croix	Knight of the Rose Croix
19°	Grand Pontiff	Grand Pontiff

chart continued on next page

Southern Jurisdiction	Northern Masonic Jurisdiction
20° Master of the Symbolic Lodge	Master *ad Vitam*
21° Noachite, or Prussian Knight	Patriarch Noachite
22° Knight of the Royal Axe, or Prince of Libanus	Prince of Libanus
23° Chief of the Tabernacle	Chief of the Tabernacle
24° Prince of the Tabernacle	Brother of the Forest
25° Knight of the Brazen Serpent	Master of Achievement
26° Prince of Mercy, or Scottish Trinitarian	Friend and Brother Eternal
27° Knight of the Sun, or Prince Adept	Knight of Jerusalem
28° Knight Commander of the Temple	Knight of the Sun, or Prince Adept
29° Scottish Knight of Saint Andrew	Knight of Saint Andrew
30° Knight Kadosh, or Knight of the White and Black Eagle	Grand Inspector
31° Inspector Inquisitor	Knight Aspirant
32° Master of the Royal Secret	Prince of the Royal Secret

The 33° has a very different ritual in both jurisdictions. The Southern Jurisdiction uses an updated version of Albert Pike's ritual, while the Northern Masonic Jurisdiction's has changed dramatically many times. In addition, the Southern Jurisdiction has additional steps required for a Scottish Rite Mason to receive the degree. There is a forty-six-month waiting period after joining the Rite in the SJ before a member may be nominated to receive the honorary rank and decoration of Knight Commander of the Court of Honor (K.C.C.H.). Only after an additional forty-six months as a K.C.C.H. can he be elected to the receive the 33°. For this reason, and others, the description in *The Lost Symbol* of Mal'akh quickly bribing his way into the 33° of the Southern Jurisdiction with a fat check to the Rite's charities, almost immediately after becoming a Mason, is not realistic, apart from being insulting. In fact, if a man asks for it, campaigns for it, or otherwise makes it clear that he's desperate to be a 33° Mason, it's almost certain he will never be nominated.

In the Northern Masonic Jurisdiction, there is only one forty-six-month requirement for eligibility to receive the 33°, and while there is a Meritorious Service Award (as well as a Distinguished Service Award), they are not required intermediate steps toward the 33°.

The number *33* was not selected at random by the originators of the Scottish Rite. It has long been considered sacred within Christianity for several reasons. It is the multiple use of three, signifying the Holy Trinity. Christ was thirty-three years old when he ascended into heaven, and the gospels list thirty-three miracles performed by Christ. However, Dan Brown is incorrect when he states, appropriately on page 333 of *The Lost Symbol*, that God is mentioned thirty-three times in the Book of Genesis. God is actually mentioned thirty-*two* times, in the first *chapter* of Genesis in the King James Bible.

Thirty-three also appears in the Old Testament and other Jewish writings. Jacob had thirty-three children; Mosaic Law required that a woman purify herself for thirty-three days after her male child was circumcised; the holy day of Lag B'Omer occurs thirty-three days after the start of Passover; and the Seal of Solomon, or Star of David, made up of two intersecting triangles, is considered a graphic representation of three plus three. It also plays a prominent role in Kabbalah.

The religions of Islam, Zoroastrianism, Buddhism, and Hinduism all associate sacred meanings with the number *33*. There are even thirty-three vertebrae in the human spine. Given its widespread usage, the number stands as a symbol of the Scottish Rite's universality as well as the perfection that every man should aspire to achieve in his soul.

Another curious aspect of the numbers *32* and *33* in regards to the Scottish Rite is that both Charleston, South Carolina, the birthplace of the Rite in 1801, and Jerusalem, the Biblical location of Solomon's Temple, lie between the 32° and 33° latitude in the Northern Hemisphere. For many years it was common for Scottish Rite officers to include the latitude of their location when writing letters, articles, or papers.

Double-Headed Eagle

The double-headed eagle depicted on the cover of *The Lost Symbol* is the principal symbol of the 33° of the Scottish Rite. It is not a "double-headed phoenix," as Brown writes when describing the tattoo on Mal'akh's chest, in which his nipples are the birds' eyes. The legendary phoenix, which rises from the ashes in Greek mythology and earlier, is not the inspiration for the eagle in Masonic iconography.

Rather, the symbol comes from an early European rite of degrees called the Order of the Royal Secret, from which the Scottish Rite descended. The Royal Secret's most advanced degree was called "The Knight of the White and Black Eagle." The French Masonic authority that issued a patent (a document that authorizes the formation of new chapters) in 1761 was called the Council of the Emperors of the East and West. They used the double-headed eagle as a heraldic device (like a logo) on their documents. It is believed that they appropriated the imagery from the period of the division of the Roman Empire into an eastern and western empire under the Byzantine emperors.[3] The image of the double-headed eagle also appears in heraldry of the Holy Roman Empire, Germany, Austria, Russia, Armenia, Albania, Serbia, and many other states and as a symbol of the Greek Orthodox Church.

The double-headed eagle of the Scottish Rite 33°, and its motto, Deus Meumque Jus, *meaning God and my right.*

What makes the image specific to the Scottish Rite is the triangle on the eagle's breast, and the number *33*, signifying the Rite's 33°. This is the image on *The Lost Symbol*'s U.S. cover. However, beneath the eagle on the cover is the motto, *Ordo ab Chao*, meaning "Order from Chaos." The correct motto of the 33° is actually *Deus meumque jus*, meaning "God and my right."

The phrase *Ordo ab Chao* actually appears on a banner in the 30° of the Scottish Rite, the "Knight Kadosh, or Knight of the White and Black Eagle," which tells the story of the Knights Templar.

Heredom

Mal'akh unscrambles the code of the stone pyramid in *The Lost Symbol* and comes up with the Greek letters for the word *Heredom*, followed by an arrow pointing downward. He mistakenly believes that it refers to the Scottish Rite's House of the Temple in Washington, D.C., and that the secret of the Masons is hidden under it at the base of a winding staircase.

Heredom is an unusual word. Scottish Rite Masons today recognize it as the title of an annual collection of papers published by the Scottish Rite Research Society, which is headquartered in the building. The society's internal material suggests that the word may have been derived from *Hieros-domos*, Greek for "Holy House," *Harodim*, Hebrew for "overseers," or perhaps *Heredum*, Latin for "of the heirs." The Masonic application of the word appeared in French Rose Croix rituals as the name of a mythical Scottish mountain, purported to be the legendary site of the first Rose Croix chapter.

There is actually a Heredom degree, although not in the Scottish Rite. The Royal Order of Scotland is a Masonic order that confers two degrees—the Heredom of Kilwinning and the Knighthood of the Rosy Cross. The order as it exists today was formed in 1753 and is headquartered in Edinburgh, Scotland. Its degrees tell the legendary whopper of how Robert the Bruce's bacon was saved in his battle against England's King Edward II at Bannockburn in 1314 by a group of Knights Templar who had been hiding out in Scotland after the order was arrested in France seven years before. Membership in the modern order is honorary, and the hereditary job of Grand Master is reserved for the king of the Scots, whenever one comes forth.

Nesta Webster, in her 1928 book *Secret Societies and Subversive Movements*, quotes a French pamphlet published in 1747 by Chevalier de Bérage as saying the mountain of Heredom is "situated between the west and North of Scotland at sixty miles from Edinburgh."[4] De Bérage claimed that the mountain was the site of the first Masonic lodge in Europe, but of course, he also claimed that it was formed by the medieval Knights Templar. One has to be careful when believing legendary origins, especially where Freemasons are concerned, and more especially when Masonic legends were being created to make one rite or jurisdiction sound more "ancient" than somebody else's—and *most* especially when the Knights Templar show up in the discussion.

The House of the Temple

The House of the Temple is without equal in the world of modern Masonic architecture. It even looks like what you'd expect the head-quarters of a secret society to look like. Its commanding facade, guarded by stone sphinxes, does indeed conceal magnificent treasures. Completed in 1916, the building and much of its interior decoration were designed by architect John Russell Pope, whose most famous design is the Jefferson Memorial. For decades, the House of the Temple has been revered and praised by the architectural community as one of the top examples in the world of the classical style. It has been open to the general public for tours since 1917.

In 1909, the Supreme Grand Inspector General of the Ancient Accepted Scottish Rite, Southern Jurisdiction, James D. Richardson, had a dream for a new headquarters. The Rite had moved from Charleston to Washington in 1870 when Albert Pike moved his law practice to the city. At first, the Rite's home was made up of a small collection of connected row houses but the fraternity soon began to outgrow these humble lodgings. Although it had less than 1,000 members nationwide immediately after the Civil War, membership began to grow by leaps and bounds, and by 1905 it had become the fastest growing fraternal organization in the United States. This was quite an accomplishment, even for the so-called "Golden Age of Fraternalism," when one out of every four adult men in America belonged to some kind of fraternal organization, and many belonged to more than one.

Richardson pushed hard for a new headquarters. Chicago's Columbian Exposition in 1893 fostered what would become a national movement to beautify American cities through the use of carefully designed public spaces and monumental, classical architecture. The City Beautiful Movement was embraced wholeheartedly in Washington, D.C., and was aided by Congress's adoption in 1901 of the McMillan Plan, a dramatic redesign of the Mall and surrounding areas to create a magnificent parklike setting for monuments that were not yet built, like the Lincoln and Jefferson memorials. Pierre L'Enfant's elegant plans had become discarded over the years, and land in the Mall had become strewn with buildings, military camps, and even stockyards. Advocates of the McMillan Plan and the City Beautiful Movement believed cities needed green space and beautiful settings, along with magnificent architecture, to improve the well-being of their citizens. In spite of Dan Brown's suggestion in *The Lost Symbol* that the classical architecture of Washington, D.C., was the vision of

The Ancient Accepted Scottish Rite Supreme Council 33° Southern Jurisdiction's headquarters, the House of the Temple.

the Founding Fathers, the truth is that the overwhelming majority of the Greco-Roman public buildings in the city were built after 1901 as a direct result of the City Beautiful Movement.

These lofty visions were not merely confined to government areas and public buildings. Private companies, churches and associations like the Masons and other fraternal groups all pitched in across the nation and planned and constructed some of the most lavish, beautiful, and impressive structures in the history of the United States in a building fever that lasted from the early 1900s until the Great Depression in 1929 ground such projects to a halt.

The design of the House of the Temple is roughly based on the legendary Mausoleum at Halicarnassus, one of the legendary Seven Wonders of the Ancient World. If it hadn't been for Richardson, the House of the Temple might have looked very different—a competing design favored by some of the Rite's officers was a replica of India's Taj Mahal.[5]

The Scottish Rite draws upon many ancient cultures and religions for its ritual ceremonies and moral teachings, and the House of the Temple similarly combines details from Greek, Egyptian, and Persian origins. Symbolism is in every crevice. As you approach the entrance, two massive seventeen-ton sphinxes guard the steps. The sphinx on the right, its eyes closed in contemplation, symbolizes wisdom, and the one on the left, its eyes wide open, symbolizes power. Look up and you'll see thirty-three Ionic columns (themselves a Masonic symbol of wisdom) supporting the upper tier, capped by what resembles a stepped pyramid. Some have attempted to make a symbolic connection between the "unfinished pyramid" on the top of the House of the Temple and the unfinished pyramid in the Great Seal of the United States, but the design is actually taken from a description of the mausoleum by the Roman author Pliny in his work *Natural History*, written almost 2,000 years ago.[6] On the top of the flat portion of the pyramid of King Mausollos's original was a sculpture of four horses and a marble chariot. The House of the Temple's flat roof has no sculpture; instead, there is a large skylight that admits light

The grand entry hall of the House of the Temple, featuring Egyptian, Assyrian, and Greek architectural details.

into the Temple Room, and plays a major role in the climax of *The Lost Symbol* and the bloody demise of Mal'akh.

Egyptian, Assyrian, Hebrew, Greek, and Roman imagery all appear in Albert Pike's versions of the Scottish Rite rituals. Consequently, the House of the Temple combines those same influences architecturally. Passing through the bronze doors, you enter a lavish hall lined by deep green marble Doric columns, ending at a grand staircase. Greek, Egyptian, and Assyrian statues, carvings and details fill the room, which is lit by tall brass sconces.

The grand staircase leads to the stunning Temple Room, once the ceremonial meeting place of the 33° Supreme Commanders of the Scottish Rite Southern Jurisdiction. Each stained-glass window is adorned with a brass sculpture celebrating illumination, the symbol for knowledge. The symbol of the order, the double-headed eagle, is frequently represented in an elongated, Egyptian style, as in the panels around the skylight.

The Temple Room is the location of the prologue scenes of *The Lost Symbol*, as well as the climactic showdown between Peter Solomon

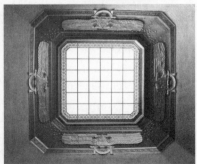

Top: The Temple Room at the House of the Temple. Middle: The black marble altar in the Temple Room. Bottom: The occulus in the ceiling over the altar.

and Mal'akh. Brown's description of the room is quite accurate. The center of the room is dominated by a black marble altar, and there is a square oculus, or skylight, directly above it, where the exterior portion of the "unfinished pyramid" roofline flattens. But Brown has taken considerable artistic license with the actual use of the room.

The 33° is not conferred in the Temple Room, and just to settle any question you might have lingering, nor is its altar used for sacrifices of humans, goats, or anything else. In most cases, the incoming class of new 33°s each year are "coroneted" in a local Washington hotel, and the degree is almost never conferred at night. The Temple Room is actually used for only a few ceremonies these days, since most of its intended purposes have outgrown the room. For their regular, nonceremonial meetings, the Supreme Council gathers in the Executive Chamber, a smaller and slightly cozier room downstairs.

In the lower levels, there are museum rooms dedicated to famous Scottish Rite Masons, and the participation of Masons in the U.S. space program. The House of the Temple is also home to the largest Masonic library in the United States, which includes Albert Pike's private collection. Many of Pike's personal effects are here as well. The Robert Burns Library is one of the finest and most complete collections of materials by and about Scotland and Freemasonry's bard.

Other specialized holdings include private collections on Abraham Lincoln, esoteric literature, and the works of the German writer and philosopher Johann Wolfgang Goethe. It is the oldest library open to the public in the District of Columbia, with more than 250,000 volumes.

The building houses a warren of offices, meeting rooms, display areas and well-guarded storage vaults. The House of the Temple is a modern-day national treasure. Built originally for $2 million, its modern worth has been estimated at $400 million.[7] Even the address of the building, 1733, is not the real street location. It was created with the help of the U.S. Post Office to interject the symbolism of thirty-three. The original mausoleum at Halicarnassus was built as the burial place for King

The remains of former Grand Commanders Albert Pike and Henry Cowles are buried in this beautiful niche in the House of the Temple. Permission was granted by an act of Congress.

Mausollos of Caria in about 350 B.C. in southwestern Turkey, in the city of known today as Bodrum. The House of the Temple is related to the ancient mausoleum in more than just design, because it houses two very real tombs. Albert Pike, the sage of the Scottish Rite's Southern Jurisdiction and its Sovereign Commander for thirty-two years, is actually buried within the building itself.

Pike lived out his last years in Washington within the Rite's previous headquarters, located at the corner of 3rd and E Streets NW. Although he had given instructions that his body be cremated and his ashes strewn around the roots of two acacia trees in front of the Supreme Council's previous home, he was buried in Oak Hill Cemetery instead. In 1944, Pike's remains were moved and placed in a vault in the House of the Temple. In 1953, Supreme Grand Commander Henry Cowles's remains were also placed in the building.

Doing so literally required special acts of Congress. It's a snooty neighborhood, and not every neighbor would be wild about having bodies buried willy-nilly up and down 16th Street.

CHAPTER 6

The Capitol Building

The U.S. Capitol building is center stage for much of the early action in *The Lost Symbol.* While it is one of the most recognized buildings in the world and a symbol of the United States, its original design was very different.

When the U.S. Constitution was adopted, it was generally believed that the heaviest concentration of power within the government of the United States was vested in the House of Representatives and the Senate because the legislative branch was thought to be closer to the will of the people. Moreover, the two houses of Congress created the laws that would govern the nation. Therefore, the position of the Capitol building was given a prominent place in the physical design of the Federal City. The L'Enfant design envisioned it on Jenkins Hill, the highest point in the city plan, both to show its predominance in the government and to symbolize that no man was above the law. He called the site, "a hill waiting for a monument."

L'Enfant was supposed to have designed the building, but he coyly claimed he had it all figured out—in his head. Whether or not that was true, it went with him when Washington fired him in 1792. The Frenchman was notoriously quarrelsome to work with and caused nothing but headaches and friction between the usually calm Washington and the new city's officials.

As with the President's House, now known as the White House, a contest was held in 1792 to choose the designer for the "Congress House," the early name for the Capitol. Most of the designs were based on Renaissance architectural forms, but the committee was unimpressed, largely because they looked too reminiscent of the existing monarchial buildings of Europe. Every one of the seventeen proposals was rejected.

A last-minute design was entered by Dr. William Thornton, a fascinating man who was born in Tortola in the British West Indies and was raised by Quakers in England. He was trained as a physician in Scotland, but it was rare that he actually practiced his profession. Instead, he dabbled as an inventor, a painter, and an architect. His proposal for the Congress House was accepted by the committee and President Washington for its "grandeur, simplicity, and convenience."

Thomas Jefferson couldn't have been happier. He favored classical Greek and Roman styles, and he was also wild about domes. Thornton's original plan featured a large domed auditorium of considerably lower profile than the one that exists today. It was also a much smaller building, though still impressive. It is easy to forget that, at the time, it needed to house the senators, representatives, and assorted sundry bureaucrats, lobbyists, and other ne'er-do-wells from a mere fifteen states.

Freemasons and the Capitol Cornerstone

While the cornerstone ceremony for the President's House had been hastily organized and performed by the Freemasons and the new city's officials with little fanfare, the city commissioners decided that the

The Masonic procession marches to the site of the cornerstone ceremony for the U.S. Capitol on September 13, 1790.

Congress House needed a much bigger kickoff ceremony. On Wednesday, September 18, 1793, President Washington crossed the Potomac and was escorted to the construction site of the President's House by members of Maryland's Lodge No. 9 and Virginia's Alexandria Lodge No. 22.

There they were joined by the members of Federal Lodge No. 15, which had just received its charter from the Grand Lodge six days before. Its Master was James Hoban, the architect of the President's House.

The assembled Masons marched "in the greatest solemn dignity, with music playing, drums beating, colors flying and spectators rejoicing," up the barely cleared road that would eventually be Pennsylvania Avenue to the little hilltop clearing that would become the symbolic center of the Federal City and the nation.[1]

A trench had been dug for the foundation, and the group took its place at the southeast corner of what would be the North Wing of the Capitol. Brother Clotworthy Stephenson, Grand Marshal, presented a silver plate to the commissioners. It read:

> This South East corner Stone, of the Capitol of the United States of America in the City of Washington, was laid on the 18th day of September 1793, in the thirteenth year of American Independence, in the first year of the second term of the Presidency of George Washington, whose virtues in the civil administration of his country have been as conspicuous and beneficial, as his Military valor and prudence have been useful in establishing her liberties, and in the year of Masonry 5793, by the Grand Lodge of Maryland, several Lodges under its jurisdiction, and Lodge No. 22, from Alexandria, Virginia.
>
> Thomas Johnson, David Stuart, Daniel Carroll, Commissioners.
> Joseph Clark, R.W.G.M.—P.T.[2]
> James Hoban, Stephen Hallate, Architects
> Collen Williamson, Master Mason[3]

After the reading of the inscription, the cornerstone was made ready. President Washington, the Grand Master *pro tempore* Joseph Clark of Maryland, and the three attending Masters of the lodges present—Elisha Cullen Dick of Alexandria No. 22, Valentine Reintzel of Maryland Lodge No. 9, and James Hoban of Federal Lodge No. 15—took the plate and stepped down into the trench. A beautiful silver trowel and marble gavel had been crafted especially for the occasion by Brother John Duffey, a silversmith in Alexandria who was a member of the president's home lodge, Fredericksburg Lodge No. 4. The trowel had a silver blade, a silver shank, and an ivory handle with a silver cap. The square was applied, a symbol of virtue, to make certain that each angle of the stone was perfectly cut. Next, the level, a symbol of equality, was used to ascertain that the stone was horizontally correct. And lastly, the plumb, an emblem of morality and rectitude, showed that the stone was perfectly upright. The stone was declared square, level, and plumb and therefore suitable as the foundation for the new building.

Kernels of wheat were sprinkled over the stone from a golden cup as a symbol of goodness, plenty, and nourishment. Wine was poured over it from a silver cup, a symbol of friendship, health, and refreshment. Finally, drops of oil glistened down its sides like the sacred oil that ran down upon Aaron's beard in the Old Testament "to the skirts of his garments; as the dew of Hermon, and as the dew that descended upon the mountains of Zion."[4] The oil symbolized joy, peace, and tranquility. The silver trowel was used to spread a small amount of cement, and the marble gavel to symbolically tap the stone into place.

George Washington in Masonic regalia at the Capitol cornerstone ceremony. Painting by Allyn Cox in the "Cox Corridor" of the Capitol.

Today, the left "valve" doors of the Senate depict a scene from the laying of the Capitol cornerstone, clearly showing Washington in his Masonic apron, and there is a fresco in the Capitol depicting the scene, as well.

Non-Masons may be especially curious about the "year of Masonry" on the cornerstone's plate—5793. One of the more confounding customs has to do with the way Freemasons date documents. The Gregorian calendar was standardized by Pope Gregory

XIII in 1582, though the non-Catholic Western world took another couple hundred years before they went along with the pope's idea. Since 1776, most of the world has been on the same calendar page, though Greece and Russia didn't adopt it until after World War I. Because Western Europe and America switched to the Gregorian calendar in the mid-1700s, conflicting ages are attributed to some of the notable figures of the period. Because of the confusion during the changeover, they themselves weren't always sure of their real age.

In 1658, Bishop James Ussher in Ireland believed he had determined the exact date of the creation of the world. Using the biblical account along with a comparison of Middle Eastern histories, Hebrew genealogy and other known events, he determined that the Earth was created on Sunday, October 23, 4004 B.C. At about the same time, John Lightfoot, vice chancellor of Cambridge University, went on to clarify that the Creation actually happened at about 9 a.m.

Ussher called his calendar *Anno Mundi*, the Year of the World. By 1700, Ussher and Lightfoot's calculations of the date and time of the Creation were accepted as fact by most Christian denominations. Beginning in 1701, new editions of the King James Bible clearly stated it right up front.

Because Ussher's Creation date was so strongly believed at the time of modern Freemasonry's origin, the Masons began dating their documents using 4004 B.C. as their beginning year . . . sort of. The number *4004* was inconvenient to remember, so Masons simply took the current year and added 4,000 to it. So, A.D. 1793 became 5793 *Anno Lucis*, or A.L., and A.D. 2007 would be 6007 A.L. *Anno Lucis* means "year of light" in Latin. Masons called it that to coincide with the Genesis passage, "And God said, 'Let there be light'; and there was light." They did this early on to lend their fraternity an air of great and solemn antiquity. If they dated their documents as being 5717 years old, they'd certainly sound more respectable and impressive than some newly formed London drinking club. Today, you will often see two dates on Masonic cornerstones—both A.D. and A.L.

The Capitol's west facade in 1839. Latrobe's dome was taller than Thornton
had called for in his original design. Made of wood and prone to leaks,
it would soon be replaced.

The U.S. Congress met in the first completed portion of the Capitol, the North Wing, in November 1800. In the 1850s, major extensions to the North and South ends of the Capitol were required because of rapid westward expansion of the country and the subsequent growth of Congress. During this expansion, the distinctive dome that makes the building so readily identifiable replaced the less grandiose, much shorter, squatter (and leaky) one that was part of Dr. Thornton's original design. Since that time, additional office buildings have been built up on streets adjacent to the Capitol to handle the needs of an ever-increasing, swollen bureaucracy.

Because of modifications to the building after it was burned in 1814 by British troops, along with expansions in the 1850s, the original cornerstone laid by George Washington and the Freemasons has been lost. In 1893, on the one hundredth anniversary of the laying of the Capitol's cornerstone, a plaque was placed near the spot where it was believed to lie. It read:

Beneath this tablet the corner stone of the Capitol of the
United States of America
was laid by
George Washington
First President September 18, 1793
On the Hundredth Anniversary
in the year 1893
In presence of the Congress the Executive and the Judiciary
a vast concourse of the grateful people
of the District of Columbia commemorated the event.
Grover Cleveland President of the United States
Adlai Ewing Stevenson Vice President
Charles Frederick Crisp Speaker, House of Representatives
Daniel Wolsey Hoorhees Chairman Joint Committee of Congress,
Lawrence Gardner Chairman Citizens Committee

In 1932, the bicentennial of George Washington's birth was celebrated across the nation. To mark the occasion, the Freemasons of Washington, D.C., dedicated a new stone at the Capitol building. Located at the Old Supreme Court Chamber entrance, on the first floor, east front, it reads:

Laid Masonically Sept. 17, 1932
in Commemoration of the Laying
of the Original Cornerstone by
George Washington

The Architect of the Capitol

Important to the story of *The Lost Symbol* is the character of Warren Bellamy, a Freemason and the Architect of the Capitol. There really is an Architect of the Capitol today, both a specific person as well as an administrative office. The actual architect is appointed for a ten-year term by the president and approved by the Senate. The office of the Architect of the Capitol is responsible to the Congress for the preservation, maintenance, and operation of not just the Capitol building itself but of twenty-nine other surrounding buildings and 450 acres of land around the Capitol. This includes the Capitol Visitor Center, the three buildings that comprise the Library of Congress complex, the Senate office buildings, the underground Congressional subway, the glass-roofed U.S. Botanical Gardens building (where Bellamy gets unceremoniously dumped in *The Lost Symbol*), the Supreme Court building, and even Congress's own power plant. Historically and symbolically, Dr. William Thornton is considered the first official Architect of the Capitol, since it was his design chosen for the original building. But it was Benjamin Latrobe, a Freemason, who was the first Architect of the Capitol, charged with its original construction and the design of its details. Ionic, Doric, and Corinthian columns are well represented all over the Capitol building, and in Masonic ritual these "Orders of Architecture" represent Wisdom, Strength, and Beauty, which are often described as "the three great pillars of Freemasonry." Freemasonry teaches that there should be "Wisdom to contrive, Strength to support, and Beauty to adorn all great and important undertakings." Columns in the vestibule outside the Senate have detailed chapiters, or capitals, that depict ears of corn, a Masonic symbol of plenty used in cornerstone ceremonies. Corn also appears in the Masonic Fellow Craft degree as part of a lesson concerning the Old Testament story of Jephthah and the death of the Ephraimites (Judges 12:5, 6). Other columns contain chapiters with tobacco leaves or magnolia blossoms. Latrobe designed these to be different from the classical forms, creating new, uniquely American columns.

The Capitol building has an enormous collection of artwork. The building itself is decorated with friezes, murals, and paintings that tell the story of the United States by depicting important moments in history or abstract representations of the philosophy of our laws and principles. Statuary has been commissioned or donated over the last two centuries to commemorate heroes or the favorite sons and daughters of a moment in time from all across the country.

The Capitol Visitor Center

Dan Brown engages in some creative architecture when it comes to the subterranean levels of the U.S. Capitol building. At one time, there were four stories of basement levels in the building. As the need for offices and storage expanded over a 200-year period, there was often as much construction below ground as there was above it. Even today, there are more than 500 rooms in the building, some no larger than a broom closet, as described in the discovery of the secret (and fictional) Chamber of Reflection in *The Lost Symbol*.

Forty years after it was proposed and after seven years under construction, the Capitol Visitor Center opened in 2009. The facility has been needed for decades because there has never been an adequate gathering place for tours. I can personally attest to the need after an embarrassing and unsuccessful attempt to charm my way into the Rayburn House Office Building after way too much coffee on a bitter cold morning, with no public restrooms anywhere in the area. The Architect

The new Capitol Visitor Center, which opened in December 2008, is where Robert Langdon enters the building in the beginning of The Lost Symbol.

of the Capitol estimates that the number of visitors to the building has risen from one million annually in 1970 to three million today.

Because there was no desire to deface the existing Capitol building with a stuck-on outbuilding, the Architect of the Capitol decided to burrow into the area under the approaching walkway east of the Capitol, facing 1st Street NE, to carve out a three-story facility that contains theaters, displays, reception rooms, and a cafeteria. Massive skylights set into the walkway above, along with the sheer size of the space, keep visitors from feeling too claustrophobic. And just as Dan Brown describes, there is a long tunnel, open to the public, that starts at the east end of the Visitor Center and pops up in the basement of the Library of Congress.

Original plans called for more than half of the underground space to be left as unfinished rooms for future needs. Congress abhors a vacuum, much less unused space, and so began filling up these empty portions of the Visitor Center. The House got a two-story hearing room, while the Senate installed small hearing rooms and a television and radio studio, complete with adjoining makeup facilities, for Senators to create messages for their voters back home. Those additions plunked another $85 million into the cost of the Visitor Center, along with creating spaces visitors will never get to visit.[5]

On the occasion of the dedication and grand opening of the Visitor Center in December 2008, Senate Majority Leader Harry Reid revealed the real reason why Congress wanted the new facility:

> "In the summer because of the heat and high humidity, you could literally smell the tourists coming into the Capitol. It may be descriptive but it's true. Well, that is no longer going to be necessary."[6]

So, visitors to the Capitol now have a beautiful and efficient facility to begin their tour of the building, where they, in turn, no longer have to smell their representatives, either.

The Apotheosis of Washington

The Capitol has been through many major enlargements, overhauls, and redesigns since its cornerstone was laid, and it looks very different today than its original designer had envisioned. Dr. Thornton intended its central dome to have a round opening, or oculus, at the top, to resemble the ancient Roman Pantheon. A very different-looking dome was completed in 1824 under architect Charles Bulfinch, without Thornton's oculus.

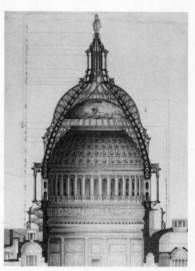

Cutaway plan of the new dome designed by Thomas U. Walter and added to the Capitol in the 1850s.

The classical Capitol dome we're used to seeing looks from the outside as though it is made of marble or plaster, but it is actually made of nine million pounds of cast iron. It was added to the building in the 1850s by Thomas U. Walter, who was inspired by St. Peter's Basilica in the Vatican. The area beneath the dome inside of the Capitol is known as the rotunda. This is the location of the scenes that touch off the excitement in *The Lost Symbol*, where the hand of Peter Solomon is discovered, pointing upward at the fresco known as *The Apotheosis of Washington*.[7] As explained by Robert Langdon in *The Lost Symbol*, the word *apotheosis* means glorification, or raising of a person to the rank of a god.

The artist Constantino Brumidi's painting *The Apotheosis of Washington* represents George Washington ascending into heaven. Washington is depicted between two female figures, one representing Liberty, the other Victory and Fame. Another thirteen women, symbolizing the original thirteen states, surround them in celebration.

Top: The Apotheosis of Washington *(1865) by Constantino Brumidi.* ***Bottom:*** "The Apotheosis of Washington *detail showing George Washington ascending to heaven.*

It was not an entirely new idea. In 1800, artist Rembrandt Peale had painted Washington floating on a cloud over Mount Vernon, being crowned with a wreath of olive branches by a winged cupid. The painting had been turned into an engraving and was popular with Americans.

Both images were undoubtedly inspired by the over-the-top description of Washington's death and "ascension" in Parson Mason Locke Weems's book, *A History of the Life and Death, Virtues and Exploits of General George Washington*, a grandiose, largely fictitious, incredibly popular book of the period:

Swift on angel's wings the brightening saint ascended; while voices more than human were warbling through the happy regions, and hymning the great procession towards the gates of heaven. His glorious coming was seen afar off; and myriads of mighty angels hastened forth, with golden harps, to welcome the honoured stranger. High in front of the shouting hosts, were seen the beauteous forms of Franklin, Warren, Mercer, Scammel, and of him who fell at Quebec, with all the virtuous patriots, who, on the side of Columbia, toiled or bled for liberty and truth . . . Their forms are of the stature of angels—their robes like morning clouds streaked with gold—the stars of heaven, like crowns, glitter on their heads—immortal youth, celestial rosy red, sits blooming on their cheeks, while infinite benignity and love beam from their eyes.[8]

The actual death of Washington was considerably quieter and less theatrical than Parson Weems's fanciful description. This isn't entirely surprising, since Weems's book was largely made up of one exaggerated howler after another—it was Weems who invented the story of Washington saying "I cannot tell a lie" after chopping down a cherry tree as a child.

Dr. Elisha Cullen Dick, a Freemason and Past Master of Washington's lodge in Alexandria, stood at his deathbed. When the president died, Dr. Dick went to the clock in the room and stopped its pendulum from swinging, preserving the moment forever. The clock is part of the museum collection at the George Washington Masonic National Memorial.

Brumidi had seen Horatio Greenough's much ridiculed 1840 statue of George Washington as Zeus, naked to the waist, with his right forefinger pointed to heaven and his left hand holding a sword. He wasn't about to put a half-nude Washington on the ceiling, and certainly not in Victorian times (although he packs the rest of the painting with a variety of naked and semi-draped cherubs, gods, and goddesses, some of whom were allegedly modeled after local Washington

prostitutes). So, Washington is painted in his military uniform, with a purple lap-blanket over his aged knees. Still, the pose in the painting is not unlike that of Greenough's statue. His right hand points down to a book of history, and his left hand holds a sword and points toward heaven. In this case, clothes made all the difference between lavish praise and hoots of derision.

Beneath the central image of Washington on his cloud

Artist Rembrandt Peale's Apotheosis of Washington *(1800).*

are scenes that represent War, Science, Marine, Commerce, Mechanics, and Architecture. They combine figures of Greco-Roman gods and goddesses with allegorical characters like Liberty, as well as modern nineteenth-century technological achievements like a steamboat and the telegraph. In the Marine scene, Neptune presides over the laying

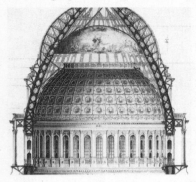

of the transatlantic telegraph cable. The War scene shows the faces of real figures from the Confederacy being vanquished, while various people involved in the construction of the new dome pop up in the Architecture and Commerce scenes.

Detail of the dome, showing the arrangement of the balcony around the base of the suspended fresco where Robert Langdon and Katherine Solomon view it up close. The now-concealed staircase up to the cupola can be seen to the left and above the concave painting.

Brumidi's 65-foot-diameter fresco took just eleven months to complete and was constructed while the greatest upheaval in U.S. history, the Civil War, was raging. The painting rises 180 feet above the floor of the rotunda, and its figures are as tall as 15 feet. The curved dome created challenges involving forced perspective so that the images looked correct from the floor as well as from the balcony that surrounds the base of the painting. At the time, gas lighting was the only light source available in the rotunda, so a space around the balcony was left as open framework so light from the windows in the cast iron dome's exterior could shine and reflect up under the painting. The open areas behind the balcony couldn't be seen from the floor, so mirrored reflectors were installed around it to bounce more light onto the painting, at least until electric lights were invented.

While access to the balcony today is heavily restricted, in *The Lost Symbol*, Robert Langdon gets access to it, as well as to the hidden staircase that passes behind the painted dome and up to the highest part of the cupola at the top of the dome, immediately beneath the feet of the

The view from the balcony under the fresco, looking down into the rotunda, that gives Robert Langdon sweaty palms.

statue of Freedom. The open spaces behind the balcony were finally walled in during the 1940s when the building was air-conditioned.

Photographs from inaugurations in the 1800s show brave onlookers perched high atop the roof and even on the dome's cupola, where only maintenance workers and security forces can visit today. And, of course, Dan Brown's Harvard professor.

The painting's placement, at the top of the rotunda dome, is directly over the crypt that lies beneath the Capitol and the rotunda's floor. Originally, there was a ten-foot-diameter hole in the floor looking into the crypt. Before George Washington's death, the plans for the Capitol included a burial vault where the president's body would be entombed forever. Washington wasn't wild about the idea himself, but the plans went ahead after he died. Washington was buried in a family crypt at Mount Vernon and, following his wishes, his family refused to allow well-meaning worshipers to move his body into the Capitol when the building was finished. The room has never been used for funerary purposes, and the observation hole was closed up in 1828 because moisture rising out of the basement level was destroying the paintings in the rotunda above. In the center of the crypt's floor is a compass rose. It marks the very center of the Federal City, the point from which all streets are numbered.

Brown's Fictional Architect and African-American Freemasonry

The fact that Dan Brown made the character of Warren Bellamy an African American and a Freemason raises an issue within Masonry's history in the United States. In spite of its stated goals of universal brotherhood among Freemasons, Masonry in the United States, like so many aspects in the society, was largely segregated for most of its history, and it constitutes a shameful mark on the Freemasons who refused to live by the tenets of the institution.

A man named Prince Hall is considered to be the father of Freemasonry in the African American community. Little is known of his early life, but most evidence today suggests that his master, William Hall of Boston, freed him from slavery after twenty-one years, and he probably took his last name from his master's household.

Prince Hall was a fascinating man. At various times he was a leather worker, soldier, civic leader, caterer, educator, property owner, and abolitionist. He fought for the establishment of schools for black children in Boston and opened a school in his own home. In 1787, as a registered voter, he successfully petitioned the Massachusetts legislature to protect free Negroes from being kidnapped and sold into slavery.

Prior to the start of the American Revolution, Prince Hall and several other black Bostonians were interested in becoming Masons and forming a lodge for other free Negroes. On March 6, 1775, Prince Hall and fourteen other black men were initiated into Lodge No. 441, an Irish military lodge attached to the 38th Foot Regiment, garrisoned at Castle William (what is now Fort Independence) in Boston Harbor. The Master of the Lodge was Sergeant John Batt, and the lodge conferred the Entered Apprentice, Fellow Craft, and Master Mason degrees on the men in one day.

The British Army fled Boston Harbor in 1776, and Prince Hall and many of his brethren joined the Revolution and enlisted in the

Continental Army. Hall himself is believed to have fought at Bunker Hill. African Lodge No. 1 survived the war and by its end had thirty-three members.

When Prince Hall and African Lodge sought a charter from the new Grand Lodge of Massachusetts after the Revolution, they were turned down. Frustrated, in 1784 African Lodge petitioned the Grand Lodge of England for a new charter. It was granted in September, but it took three years for the charter to be delivered to Boston. On May 6, 1787, the lodge officially became Lodge No. 459 of the Grand Lodge of England.

No one knows whether the decision was out of true Masonic brotherly love and friendship or just an opportunity for the Grand Master of England (who just happened to be the Duke of Cumberland and the brother of King George III) to annoy the Americans by authorizing a new lodge of black men on American soil. African Lodge forwarded its annual dues payments to London each year, but repeated communication to the Grand Lodge after receiving the charter was ignored and unanswered for years. In 1792, after being visited by black Freemasons from Pennsylvania and Rhode Island, African Lodge authorized the creation of a lodge in each of those states, under authority of its English charter.

African Lodge was stricken off the rolls of the Grand Lodge of England in 1813 after its annual dues payments stopped arriving in London—not surprising, since England and America were at war with each other again. The lodge tried one last time in 1824 to request clarification of its status and a renewed charter from London, but this request, like all the earlier ones, was ignored.

After years of continued silence from London, in 1827 African Lodge declared itself to be its own grand lodge, as most of the grand lodges in the new United States had done after the Revolution. In honor of its founder, it was eventually renamed Prince Hall Grand Lodge, and today there are approximately 200,000 members in forty-five independent jurisdictions. Interestingly, Prince Hall Grand Lodge remains the only American Masonic body still in possession of its charter from England, and it predates most of the other grand lodges in the United States.

A "separate but equal" Masonic universe has grown and thrived in America almost since the nation's beginnings. Prince Hall Freemasonry has been a proud and vibrant part of the African American social community since its beginnings and remains so today.

Over the centuries, the predominantly white grand lodges have made various claims about the legitimacy of Prince Hall's "freeborn" status, the origin of his membership, the history of African Lodge's charter, and the authenticity of its documents, all in an effort to discredit or ignore the existence of Prince Hall Freemasonry. It was not until 1989 that mainstream and Prince Hall Grand Lodges across the United States began to officially recognize each other, even though there are already black mainstream Masons and white Prince Hall Masons. The two sides have remained largely separated as a matter of choice, even after joint recognition has occurred.

In Washington, D.C, the Grand Lodge of Free and Accepted Masons of the District of Columbia has a very diverse membership base, because of the international nature of the business of the city. There are lodges that meet using foreign languages, rituals, and customs, and no two lodges in the district are alike.

In 2008, the Grand Lodge of D.C. elected Kwame Acquaah, an attorney originally from Ghana, as the first black Grand Master of a mainstream (not Prince Hall) lodge in the United States.[9] So in reality, it wouldn't be unusual for Warren Bellamy to be a member of either a Prince Hall or mainstream lodge in Washington, D.C.

Sadly, institutionalized segregation continues to exist in small pockets of U.S. Freemasonry. As of 2009, official recognition between Prince Hall and mainstream Freemasonry has been settled by all but eleven state grand lodges in the United States—and apart from West Virginia, all are among the states of the old Confederacy: Alabama, Arkansas, Georgia, Mississippi, Florida, Kentucky, Tennessee, South Carolina, Louisiana, and West Virginia.[10] The situation remains an embarrassment to the rest of the Masonic world.

CHAPTER 7

The Washington Monument

>⊓□　∀⌐∪⊓⌐⊙⊓>⊏⊙　⊐⊏⊙<⊐□□>

A clue to the end of *The Lost Symbol* can be found on the spine of the hardback edition's cover: a tiny picture of the Washington Monument is seen through a stylized keyhole. In the book, the airplane carrying Robert Langdon lands at Dulles Airport outside of Washington, but on the approach to the city, he sees the Washington Monument out of the window of the plane. That's unlikely to happen, with Dulles more than twenty miles away and post-9/11 air traffic restrictions, but the Capitol building and the Washington Monument are unquestionably the two most recognizable landmarks in the city.

The Washington Monument winds up as the location of the "lost word" Mal'akh has been hunting throughout the story. Peter Solomon reveals it to Robert Langdon in the unusual manner of blindfolding him and taking him to the top of the Monument at night (while apparently shaking off any debilitating effects having his hand amputated earlier in the evening might have caused). The world's most identifiable obelisk is the location for one of the most philosophical discussions in the book.

In 1783, the Continental Congress proposed that an equestrian statue be erected in honor of the commanding general who would soon become the first president of the United States. Not unlike everything else Congress touches, the job of building a monument to George Washington would take more than a hundred years to complete, cost millions more than what was anticipated, and look nothing like what was proposed in the first place.[1]

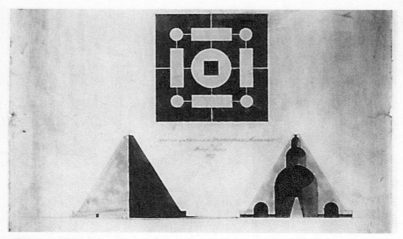

Former Mayor Peter Force's proposed monument to George Washington, shaped like an unfinished pyramid (1833). At the top was an open oculus so light could shine down into the vaulted crypt. At the time, the pyramids of Egypt were the oldest known surviving human structures on Earth, so pyramids were considered eternal symbols of timeless strength.

When Pierre L'Enfant drew up the plans for the area south of the President's House and west of the Capitol, with Washington's approval he drew in a spot for "the equestrian statue of George Washington, a monument voted in 1783 by the late Continental Congress." If you look at the street plan of the city, the monument was supposed to be exactly at the right-angle corner of a triangle formed by the White House, the Capitol building, and the monument itself. A little soggy ground altered those plans a bit, but the monument's location was symbolically placed so that presidents and members of Congress would look out of their respective buildings and gain inspiration from the memory of George Washington.

After Washington's death in December 1799, Congress spent the next fifty years proposing, studying, and rejecting several plans for a monument to Washington, each one more lavish than the last. "George perched on a horse" was just too small an idea. A committee formed in 1800 suggested a tomb shaped like an enormous pyramid, echoing the unfinished pyramid on the reverse of the Great Seal of the United States. Ideas continued to come in over the years, many of them incorporating pyramids or other Egyptian-themed designs. Napoleon's modern, scientific invasion of Egypt in 1798, with his troops and warships accompanied by historians and artists, had helped make Egyptian motifs very popular. Former mayor Peter Force suggested a particularly spectacular pyramid monument with an "unfinished" top and an oculus that emitted light down into the interior of the vault. It seemed that the gentleman farmer, general, and president might end up being made a pharaoh, after all.

Finally, a group of private citizens formed the Washington National Monument Society in 1833 to create a design and raise money for its construction.[2] An appeal was made to every state in the nation, and donations were limited to no more than one dollar a year per person to insure that they came from the hearts of all of the people and not just from fat-cat donors. A nice sentiment but an impractical financial plan—the money came in at a trickle until the restriction was lifted.

A design was submitted to the new Monument Society by Robert Mills, a Freemason from South Carolina. Mills had been appointed in 1836 as the country's first federal architect by President Andrew Jackson, so he had an inside track on the commission. Mills's first plan was for a huge, circular temple, made up of thirty massive 100-foot-tall columns and topped by an Egyptian obelisk 600 feet tall—45 feet higher than the present structure. Mills saw the temple much like the Pantheons in Paris and Rome. He envisioned that it would be surrounded with statues of the Founding Fathers: the signers of the Declaration of Independence and war heroes. Over the entry to the

Robert Mills's plan for the Washington Monument (1836).

temple was to be a sculpture of Washington himself, facing the east, riding in a horse-drawn chariot like Helios bringing forth the dawn. Mills's design combined Greek, Roman, Egyptian, and Babylonian architecture and was something of an overblown train wreck of styles. Aesthetically, it was a nightmare, with very few defenders. Worse, Mills's proposed price tag came to $1 million in 1836 dollars, which would be about $17 million today. It was a little ambitious for a group that had raised only $28,000.

It took another twelve years for the society to collect $87,000, but it was enough for Congress to finally take them seriously and grant them the thirty-seven-acre plot of land L'Enfant had put in his plan. Unfortunately, the Mills design, even if reduced in size, didn't have a chance of standing there. Simply put, the property was a mud-sucking bog. After some exploration, it was determined that the land one hundred yards to the south was dry enough and sturdy enough to support the monument, so geometric symmetry gave way to practicality.

The plan was to build the obelisk first. Mills shortened its height to 500 feet to cut costs, but it still called for a 250-foot-diameter colonnade made up of 100-foot-tall columns, which would be added when the central shaft was completed. Mills was clearly far more enraptured by the details of the pantheon, and he described it in excruciating detail. The obelisk had a flatter top than its present design, and the four sides were to be inscribed with Washington's greatest achievements. On the side of the obelisk facing the east, near the top, was to be a five-pointed star "emblematic of the glory which the name of Washington has attained."[3]

The obelisk, a design first fashioned by the ancient Egyptians, is thought to have been inspired by the rays of the sun. Most ancient Egyptian obelisks were dedicated to the sun god Ra, and twenty-seven of them have survived to the present day. You can see several of these obelisks all over the world; they were looted by the European powers that conquered Egypt over the centuries and installed in their own capitals of London, Paris, and Istanbul. There's even one in New York, an 1879 gift of the pasha of Egypt to the United States. Unlike its

Egyptian predecessors, the Washington Monument was not carved out of a solid slab of rock and raised in one piece. It was built of white marble stones. The cornerstone for the Washington Monument was laid on the Fourth of July in 1848, sixty-five years after Congress had first approved the idea. The brethren of Washington Naval Lodge No. 4 helped drag the massive white marble block to the job site from the railroad depot four blocks away. Some 20,000 people watched as President James K. Polk led a parade to the site of the monument.[4] Benjamin B. French, Grand Master of the Grand Lodge of Washington, D.C., approached the stone wearing George Washington's Masonic sash and apron, which had been given to him by General Lafayette, and he used Washington's gavel to set the cornerstone. It was the same Masonic regalia and gavel that Washington had used to dedicate the cornerstone of the Capitol building.

By 1855, the obelisk had risen 155 feet, but then reality stepped in. To get this far had cost $300,000, and the Monument Society had run out of money. In February, they appealed to Congress, which finally stepped up and voted to partially fund the monument they had recommended seventy years before. Meanwhile, the society sent out the word to the states, again looking for help. Alabama hit upon a novel idea—the donation of a "state stone," a suitably inscribed block of stone native to its state. The idea generated enthusiastic press, and soon states, clubs, associations, labor unions, foreign nations, and private citizens were contributing inscribed blocks to be used for the interior

Construction stopped in 1855 at the 155-foot level. The difference in the white marble stones makes a distinct line that can be seen today.

walls, where they can be seen today throughout the monument. The stone from Alaska is the most valuable. It is made of solid green jade and valued at several million dollars. At least twenty-two stones were donated by Masonic lodges and grand lodges across the country.[5]

One of the stones caused a major scandal. In 1854, Pope Pius IX donated a block of marble from the Temple of Concord in Rome. During this dark period in American racial politics, the Nativist movement was growing in popularity. Nativists—American-born Protestants who had a particular dislike and distrust of Catholics— believed that new waves of Irish immigration would result in America becoming a Catholic country controlled by the pope through his faithful surrogates. "Anti-popery" swept the nation, just as anti-Masonry had done nearly three decades before. Pius IX, who had earlier opposed liberties in the Papal States that Americans had fought hard to win—especially freedom of religion—was increasingly seen as a tyrant by Protestants. It didn't help matters that he defined the concepts of Immaculate Conception and the infallibility of the Holy Father when speaking on matters of faith; neither idea had yet been hardened into canon law. Protestants worldwide reacted violently to both pronouncements as heresy. So, the arrival of the pope's stone at the memorial job site was a case of extremely bad timing.

One night, a group of ten members of the Know-Nothing Party, a Nativist political group, broke into the construction yard and stole the pope's stone. Rumor had it that they dumped it into the Potomac. Others speculated that it was dumped into a power company job site or ground into powder and used as part of the monument's mortar mix. A replacement stone was sent and is part of the monument today.

The Know-Nothing Party was created as a secret society, and many believe it had substantial Masonic membership. As a political party, it enjoyed a brief period of popularity in the 1850s. One of the Know-Nothings' most outlandish actions was to seize the Washington Monument. Through a carefully orchestrated rigging of the election of Monument Society members, the Know-Nothings took over the board. After four years of Know-Nothing control, nothing much was accomplished, and Congress took its $200,000 back. It would put no more money into the project for another twenty years.

The Know-Nothings eventually deserted the monument as well, and construction stopped completely in 1861, leaving the 176-foot-high stump looking "like a hollow, oversized chimney," to quote Freemason Mark Twain.[6] During the Civil War, the area around the monument became a cattle yard and slaughterhouse to supply provisions for Union troops.

In 1876, with the war over and the centennial of the Declaration of Independence approaching, Congress finally appropriated $2 million to finish the job. The base was found to be insufficient for the weight of the completed structure and had to be modified before it could rise farther. And there was still that pantheon to be built.

A lawyer named George Peter Marsh finally brought everyone to their senses. As the U.S. minister to Italy, he had made a study of the art of obelisks. His recommendation was to scrap the pantheon, columns, and statuary of Mills's original design and concentrate on just the elegant obelisk. Work began anew. The foundation was enlarged, hiding the cornerstone forever, and the obelisk again began to rise.

In 1851 and 1853, the original Monument Society had solicited contributions from the Freemasons nationally through the grand lodges, knowing the fraternity's long association with Washington. So the call went out again in 1874, and pledges were received from Masons all over the country, as well as from non-Masonic fraternal bodies like the Odd Fellows, the Knights of Pythias, and the Improved Order of Red Men. In 1875, more than two hundred Masonic lodges across the country responded to the appeal.

By 1884, the main body of the monument was completed. The difference in the age and quarry source of the marble can still be seen at the old 155-foot level today, marked by a slight difference in color. The top of the monument had been changed from Mills's flatter outline to a more sharply peaked pyramidion in the 1870s redesign. To more closely resemble the element in the Great Seal, the pyramid was made up of thirteen rows of marble. The stonecutters dressed the stones of the final peak on the ground and then hoisted it into place in one piece.

Before being delivered to Washington, the aluminum capstone was placed on display in Tiffany's in New York, and patrons were

given the chance to "jump over the Washington Monument." At the time, aluminum was an extremely rare metal, as expensive as silver but more durable. This was long before our present-day image of it as something to drink beer out of or wrap around turkeys. It was inscribed with the Latin words *Laus Deo*, meaning "Praise God," on one side. In case there had ever been a question about the symbol of the All-Seeing Eye atop the pyramid of the Great Seal being sinister, this made it clear: the capstone of both the seal and this

The aluminum capstone was hoisted to the top of the Monument and set into place on December 6, 1884. Inscribed on its face are the words "Laus Deo."

monument was no occult symbol but an image of God's omniscience watching over us and guiding the nation.

Because the original cornerstone at the base had been buried, the aluminum capstone would become a new focal point. It was hoisted to the top of the 555-foot tower—in sixty-mile-an-hour winds—and set into place with Masonic ceremonies on December 6, 1884, one hundred and one years after Congress had proposed it.

A scandal recently erupted when a reproduction of the aluminum capstone was put on display at the 490-foot level of the monument. It was shoved against a wall in such a way that the words *Laus Deo* could not be seen by the public. Either by accident or by design, it certainly looked like the reference to praising God was turned away so as not to offend those who believe proclamations of faith have no place on public buildings. Reinforcing that sentiment, a new plaque next to the capstone had deliberately removed any reference to *Laus*

Deo or any mention of God. After a noisy protest, the display was rearranged and reworded.[7]

Obelisks are fascinating geometric sculptures, but they are not without controversy. It wouldn't take Sigmund Freud, or even Dr. Phil, very long to peg the obelisk as a phallic symbol, and there are those who suggest that the Washington Monument is an occult icon for that reason. The "Egyptian sun god" reference makes others uneasy. Still, it must be remembered that Washington was revered for decades as a godlike character, and no amount of veneration in a monument to him was considered excessive. Connecting the general and president with a divine entity that cast the warmth of his rays on the citizenry, along with displaying 555 feet of virile potency capable of fathering a nation, probably sounded like a laudable idea at the time. There is no mistaking the awe-inspiring vision it instills the first time you see the monument in person, in a way that no statue ever could.

Above all, there is the simple timelessness of the monument's design. Robert Mills believed that the most important part of his proposal was the pantheon of heroic figures who founded the nation, with the president himself ready to leap into the sky and race across the heavens in his chariot like the Greek god Apollo. But Washington himself would have recoiled at such hero worship preserved forever in marble, like the world's most expensive kitsch, the modern-day equivalent of a painting on black velvet. It was scarcely the "general-on-a-horse" type of thing that he, Congress, and L'Enfant had envisioned. The Washington Monument succeeds as art, as a landmark, and as a symbol of the importance of his position in

The Washington Monument today.

America, without impressing an image on us. The paintings of him have been exposed to interminable armchair analysis. (He looks mad. He looks old. His hair looks funny. Why is he in a toga? Was he wearing his wooden false teeth?) The monument avoids that and remains ageless, immune to false interpretations.

In his own monument, George Washington himself is relegated to little more than a statue in an alcove on the ground floor—almost an afterthought. If you never go into the monument, you never see old George. What is seen is the idea. *Laus Deo*. Praise God.

In a scene in *The Lost Symbol,* Robert Langdon descends through the monument in the glass-windowed elevator, looking at the many commemorative stones that were donated from all over the world. Some of the 193 stones come from Masonic lodges and grand lodges. But they also come from other civic groups, churches, labor organizations, all collected together in this one place, side by side. In a way, it is a metaphor in stone to the notion of putting aside differences to build something for the ages. It's almost Masonic.

CHAPTER 8

Myths, Legends, and Dan Brown's Washington

⅃<>ᑎᐯ, ᄂᄀᓚᄀᑐᑐᑐ, ᒍᐤᒍ
ᑐᒍᄆ ᑌ⌐ᒪᐯᄆ'ᐯ ᐱᒍᐯᑎᄀᄀ⁊>ᑕᑐ

In *The Lost Symbol*, Dan Brown uses a short sequence in a taxi to slaughter some of the most sacred cows of Masonic lore about the capital of the United States. In an attempt to elude chase by the CIA, Katherine Solomon plays a game of connect-the-dots on the back of a dollar bill to spell "MASON" and send a deliberately wrong message to eavesdropping CIA agents. Then, in a scene at Freedom Plaza on Pennsylvania Avenue, where the Federal Triangle of the city is laid out in a large-scale, walkable map, she and Robert Langdon send the bungling agents the wrong way—to the George Washington Masonic Memorial, across the Potomac River in Alexandria, Virginia. While the CIA agents race off to the south in their helicopter, the two intrepid heroes head north to the National Cathedral.

Throughout *The Lost Symbol*, the nation's capital is almost a secondary character, and many of its prominent buildings help to propel the mystery forward. So here's a brief tour of Washington's landmarks that play starring or walk-on roles in the book.

The "Masonic" Map

For the last twenty years or so, the world of esoteric researchers and conspiracy lovers alike have been gazing into the geometric patterns of the map of Washington, D.C., in search of sinister or occult patterns. Inventive "researchers" have spotted Satanic pentagrams, devilish goat heads, Masonic squares and compasses, Jewish Stars of David, clues linked to Baal and Moloch, and pagan horned owls. More skeptical cartographers have also spotted an ice cream cone and an evil dachshund. Where once the world had seen a Baroque plan of broad, radial avenues, ceremonial spaces and respectful use of existing topography, these people now see only a Freemason plot—a Federal City designed to boast of the influence of its secret Masonic masters.

Unfortunately for all of these overly imaginative folks, Freemasons do not worship, venerate, or otherwise prostrate themselves to symbols. On the contrary, Freemasonry celebrates reason, science, learning, and freedom from superstition. Symbolism is primarily used as a memory device or an allegory to teach a moral lesson. But such trivial details have never kept a good conspiracy theory down.

David Ovason's book, *The Secret Architecture of Our Nation's Capital*, was first published in 1999 under the title *The Secret Zodiacs of Washington, D.C.: Was the City of Stars Planned by Masons?* In both

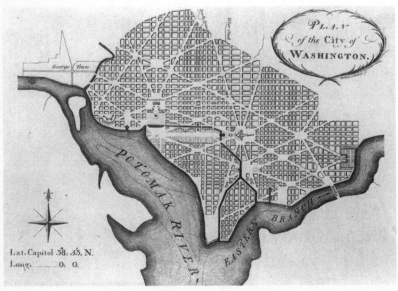

The L'Enfant Plan of the Federal City (1791).

cases, the title and packaging imply that there's something "secret" or even creepy about the building of Washington—and that the Masons must have put it there.

The city map of Washington, D.C., originally designed by Pierre L'Enfant and Andrew Ellicott, is a true work of mathematical art. Anyone who has visited a very old European city knows what the new city planners were rebelling against. George Washington, in his own diaries and exchanges with the bitter and embattled L'Enfant, as well as with Thomas Jefferson, made it clear that he cared little about the arrangement of streets, squares, and roundabouts. Washington was interested solely in the placement of the Capitol building and the President's House because of their symbolic juxtaposition, each on a hill overlooking the city. A broad, panoramic street, Pennsylvania Avenue, connected them so that the Congress and the president could symbolically watch what each other was up to, while both looked out over the city.

L'Enfant and Ellicott were not Masons, so designing any sort of Masonic symbolism into the street plans of the city would have been a neat trick for them. Ovason claims L'Enfant was a Mason but admits in an endnote that his alleged source material was a previously "unpublished manuscript," which has not yet been published nearly a decade later.[1] As to Ellicott, he says, "Although I have no doubt that Ellicott was a Mason, I have not been able to discover to which lodge he belonged."[2] The book is rife with such speculation presented as fact.

In the end, Ovason comes to a conclusion that contradicts virtually everything else in his book: "I am not suggesting for one moment that it was 'the Masons who built Washington, D.C.,' or that Masons' Lodges ever had a coordinated, formulated plan to influence the growth of the city in any way."[3]

One of the most common assertions concerning the design of Washington, D.C., has to do with the supposed inverted pentagram that appears in the street plan over the White House. The accusation is that the inverted pentagram was placed there by the Masonic

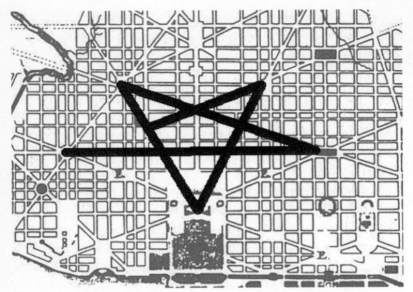

The unfinished pentagram in the streets north of the White House.
From the L'Enfant Plan (1791).

designers of the nation's capital as an occult talisman to show their
mysterious power over the government. Or something like that.

The pentagram, or five-pointed star, is a common symbol. It
appears fifty times on the American flag, though conspiracy theorists
have apparently overlooked this occult symbol apparently placed on
our flag by that pagan witch Betsy Ross and her dark overlord George
Washington during one of their Satanic sewing bees.

The pentagram has occasionally appeared in the symbolism of
Freemasonry, most prominently as the symbol of the Order of the
Eastern Star, part of the Masonic family of related groups known as
the appendant bodies. The order was created in the 1850s by
Freemason Rob Morris and his wife as a group that allowed both men
and women to mix in a lodge-like setting. The pentagram as used in
the Order of the Eastern Star represents the Star of Bethlehem.
Chapter rooms are traditionally laid out with a large floorcloth or car-
pet representing the pentagram and its star points. At the center of the
symbol stands an altar with an open Bible upon it.

Apart from its use in the Order of the Eastern Star, the penta-gram—right side up or inverted—does not officially appear in U.S. Masonic ritual or symbolism. Some "tracing boards" (painted symbol-ism charts used to teach Masonic lessons) in the early 1800s con-tained five-pointed stars with a letter *G* in the center as a symbol of both God and geometry. Other researchers have suggested that it may have represented a portion of the Master Mason degree ritual, the "Five Points of Fellowship." But it was not a common symbol and has not survived in widespread use.

The inverted pentacle wasn't an inherently "evil" symbol when Pierre L'Enfant was alive. The first mention of pentagrams being "good" or "evil" appeared more than sixty years after L'Enfant designed the street plan for Washington, D.C., in Eliphas Lévi's book, *Dogme et rituel de la haute magie* (Doctrine and Ritual of High Magic), published in 1855.

The real question is whether the pentagram actually appears in Washington's street plan at all. The answer is, sort of . . . but not really. Look at the map of the streets north of the White House. Using the White House as the bottom point, trace Connecticut Avenue to DuPont Circle; Massachusetts Avenue to Mt. Vernon Square; K Street back west to the circle at 23rd Street; and then—nothing. The final leg of the pentagram is supposed to be Rhode Island Avenue, traced to Vermont Avenue and then back to the White House, the "evil" tip of the inverted point. But Rhode Island Avenue doesn't extend between 23rd Street and Connecticut Avenue, and there is no evidence that it was ever supposed to connect. As Masonic author Dr. S. Brent Morris has pointed out, if the Masons were all-powerful, wouldn't they have finished the job so this unholy talisman could achieve full potency?

The Square and Compass and the Capitol

Similar claims have been made that the streets around the Capitol building outline a Masonic square and compass. The "square" is formed by Louisiana Avenue and Washington Avenue. The "top" of the compass is the Capitol itself, with its two legs stretching down Pennsylvania Avenue to the White House and, in a broken, meandering way, along Maryland Avenue toward the Jefferson Monument. One problem: there is no Masonic significance to the Jefferson Monument, since Jefferson is not known to have been a Mason. There's also a problem with the supposed mystical symbolism of a Masonic connection between the White House and the Capitol. To the east of the White House, an obstruction to this "sacred line" was built in 1836—at the order of a Masonic president. Freemason Andrew Jackson ordered the new Treasury building to be built next to the White House, slicing across Pennsylvania Avenue, to block his view of Congress, with whom he was at political loggerheads. As a Past Grand Master of Tennessee, perhaps Jackson should have known better, but maybe he wasn't at the lodge meeting the night his brethren discussed preserving the magic Masonic line between the White House and the Capitol.

Drawing lines all over a map of Washington is like eating popcorn. There are a half dozen pentagrams, at least two instances of the six-pointed Seal of Solomon (Star of David), and countless square and

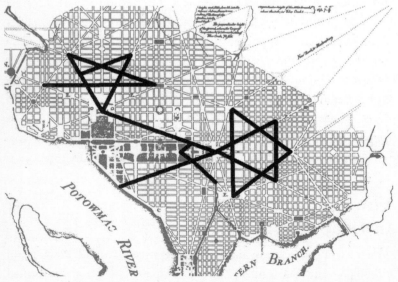

The supposed Masonic symbolism in the streets of Washington.
From the L'Enfant Plan (1791).

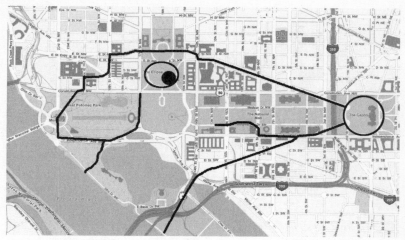

There are pentagrams and a Seal of Solomon in the map of Washington, D.C.
As writer Steve Reed discovered, there's also an evil dachshund.
Stare at the map long enough and you'll find all kinds of shapes.

compass patterns. You get even more if you cheat with streets that don't go through, as the purveyors of these nonsensical claims do. It is a function of diagonal lines laid down over a north-south gridline. The same patterns can be found in the maps of Paris, Rome, Detroit, and Baghdad.

Masons in the Dollar

Congress appointed a committee in 1776 to design a seal for the new nation, to be used as the official "signature" of the country on documents, laws, and treaties. The four men on the first committee were Benjamin Franklin, John Adams, Thomas Jefferson, and the only true artist among them, Pierre du Simitière. Of the four men, only one, Franklin, was a Mason. His suggestion to the committee was that the seal depict a scene from Exodus. It would show Moses causing the parted waters of the Red Sea to destroy the oncoming chariots of Pharaoh's approaching army, while a pillar of fire reaches down from the heavens. His suggested motto was "Rebellion to Tyrants Is Obedience to God."

Left: Benjamin Franklin's proposal for the Great Seal of the United States, depicting Moses and the Hebrews escaping Egypt as the Red Sea destroys Pharaoh and his army (1777). *Right:* Pierre du Simitière's proposal for the Great Seal of the United States (1777).

Thomas Jefferson's suggestions had a similar Old Testament theme. The front of his two-sided seal would show the children of Israel in the wilderness, being led to the Promised Land by a bright cloud in the day and a pillar of fire at night. The reverse of his seal would have shown Horsa and Hengist, two legendary Anglo-Saxon leaders in ancient Britain.

John Adams turned to the classics for inspiration. He proposed an image of Hercules leaning on a large club, with the figure of Virtue on his right and Sloth on his left—the Greek equivalent of an angel on one shoulder and a devil on the other.

Du Simitière went a different route. His was a more standard European-style shield or coat of arms, divided into six sections to represent America's roots in England, Scotland, Ireland, France, Germany, and Holland, surrounded by thirteen smaller shields representing the original thirteen states. On the left side of the shield was a figure of Liberty, wearing armor and holding a spear in one hand. On the other was an anchor, a symbol of hope (which, by the way, does appear in Masonic symbolism with the same meaning). On the right side was a frontiersman, wearing buckskin and holding a tomahawk. Surrounding this design were the only elements from this committee that would make it to the final design. Above the shield was an All-Seeing Eye in a triangle, beaming down rays of light. Below the shield was the motto, *E Pluribus Unum* (Out of Many, One), and the Roman numerals for 1776, MDCCLXXVI.

Robert Hieronimus's book, *Founding Fathers, Secret Societies*, presents one of the most detailed historical accounts of the Great Seal of the United States. In it, Hieronimus suggests that Du Simitière actually cribbed the motto from the title page of a contemporary London publication, *Gentleman's Magazine*.

Congress didn't think much of the committee's recommendations, so it did what congresses do best—it formed another committee. One member of the second group was Francis Hopkinson, an artist who had designed the first American flag, several official seals, and some colonial currency. Hopkinson added the idea of an unfinished pyramid based on a fifty-dollar note he had designed in 1778. It should be noted that Hopkinson was not a Mason, either.

A third committee at last finalized the design in 1782, using elements from several different proposals, and this is the seal that appears on the back of the dollar bill today. The items most cited as being "Masonic" were explained by William Barton, an artistic consultant brought in by the committee.

> The Pyramid signified Strength and Duration: The Eye over it & the Motto allude to the many signal interpositions of providence in favor of the American cause. The date underneath is that of the Declaration of Independence and the words under it signify the beginning of the new American Era, which commences from that date.[4]

Both mottoes that appear on the reverse of the seal were contributed to the design by Charles Thompson, a member of the third committee. The Latin inscription *Annuit Coeptis* translates as "He (God) has favored our undertakings" and refers to God's assistance in the creation of the new nation. The inscription *Novus Ordo Seclorum* translates as "A New Order of the Ages" and signifies the new Ameri-

The reverse side of the Great Seal of the United States as it appears on the one-dollar bill.

Forming the anagram "MASON" from the motto.

Joining the letters that make the Mason anagram with the All-Seeing Eye creates the Seal of Solomon.

can era. It does not, as has been often suggested, mean "New World Order." Nor does it mean "Secular World Order," as fundamentalist Christians have suggested.

Of all the fourteen men who had a hand in the design of the Great Seal of the United States, only Benjamin Franklin was a Mason, and not one of his design elements made it into the final version. Although the influential social critic Charles Eliott Norton declared at the time that the reverse of the seal is "a dull emblem of a Masonic fraternity," it is nothing of the kind. Norton was most likely making a snide artistic judgment, not an anti-Masonic accusation. Nevertheless, his comment is the likely source of the notion that the back of the dollar bill contains Masonic symbols.

Now, let's look at that scene in *The Lost Symbol* where Katherine Solomon pulls out a dollar bill and decrypts the word *MASON* on it. This is how it's done: Circle the *A* in *Annuit*, the *S* in *Coeptis*, the *N* in *Novus*, the *M* in *Seclorum*, and the second *O* in *Ordo*. Rearrange those letters, *ASNMO*, and they spell *MASON*. Is it possible that Charles Thompson intended this anagram to be hidden in the mottoes he suggested, even if he wasn't a Mason himself?

Now, draw a line from the tip of the eye down to the *N*, over to the *M*, and back to the eye. Connect another line from the *A* to the *S*, down to the *O*, and back to the *A*. The lines form a hexagram, a six-pointed star better known as the Star of David or the Seal of Solomon.

Of course, the following anagrams also appear in the motto: onerous, ottoman, despots, sopranos, semiconductors, radioisotopes, uncircumcised, Micronesians, accordionists, autoeroticism, and most significantly, misconception.

Conspiracy lovers and those who get the creeps over the "occult" number *13* may point out the thirteen rows of bricks in the pyramid. Like the thirteen stripes in the U.S. flag, there is nothing occult about their presence. They stand for the original thirteen colonies that formed the United States. Others assert that the date 1776 is there to commemorate not the signing of the Declaration of Independence but the founding in Bavaria of the Illuminati, the centerpiece organization of Dan Brown's *Angels & Demons*. To some folks, the entire image is proof that the Illuminati are alive and well and in control of the U.S. government. It would at least be reassuring to think that somebody is.

The George Washington Masonic Memorial

In *The Lost Symbol*, Robert Langdon and Katherine Solomon dupe the CIA into thinking they have hightailed it to the George Washington Masonic Memorial in Alexandria, Virginia. Located at the corners of King and Callahan Streets, it is right where Dan Brown says it is: directly across the street from the King Street Blue Line Metro station. It's hard to miss. Standing 333 feet tall, the memorial is built on the highest point in Alexandria, Shuter's Hill. On the hillside in front of the impressive structure, a colossal square and compass is set into the landscaping, almost large enough to spot from low-Earth orbit.

In 1911, a meeting took place at Alexandria-Washington Lodge No. 22 in Alexandria, Virginia, in a room over City Hall. The lodge was in possession of artifacts from President Washington's life, especially from the moment of his death at Mount Vernon. These were priceless relics, and the lodge wanted to create a museum to display and protect them. They had good reason to worry.

George Washington was named as the first Master of Alexandria Lodge No. 22 when it received its charter from the Grand Lodge of Virginia after the Revolution, in 1788, even though he never actually presided over a meeting there. In 1804, the lodge was officially allowed to incorporate his name and the lodge was renamed Alexandria-Washington Lodge No. 22. The lodge had in its possession many personal effects of the president, and it collected more in subsequent years. Then, in 1871, the lodge building burned, and some of their collection was lost. By the time of the meeting at City Hall in 1911, the lodge knew a safer location was the only solution to protecting the irreplaceable heirlooms, and a national movement began to grow in favor of more than just a small museum.

The George Washington Masonic Memorial in Alexandria, Virginia.

On May 22, 1932, the George Washington Masonic Memorial was dedicated. It was grander than anything the men who assembled in 1911 had ever dreamed. In spite of the individual sovereignty of the grand lodges in each state, this remains the only national project built with the participation of all of them. Unlike the more famous public monument in Washington, D.C., this one was erected in just ten years, entirely from the contributions of American Freemasons.

Like the legendary lighthouse that adorned the harbor of Alexandria in ancient Egypt, this modern-day "lighthouse" holds cherished relics and knowledge of the fraternity. The centerpieces of the memorial include the bronze statue of Washington in the colonnaded Memorial Hall, with murals depicting the cornerstone ceremony of the Capitol, and General Washington with his officers at Christ Church in Philadelphia during a St. John's Day Observance on December 28, 1788. There is an extensive museum filled with artifacts relating to Washington, sponsored by the Southern and Northern Masonic Jurisdictions of the Scottish Rite. The memorial's library contains more than 20,000 volumes of Masonic and related works.

The Memorial is home to two lodges that meet regularly, plus a lodge of research and at least seven other Masonic groups. Alexandria-Washington Lodge No. 22 has recreated a lodge room from the period during which Washington was a member. It is a replica of the room in Old Town Alexandria where members met for many years. The lodge today meets in a separate room in the memorial. Andrew Jackson Lodge No. 120 meets in the North Lodge Room, a differently styled chamber with Gothic details.

The various affiliated organizations of Freemasonry contributed to the memorial as well, and several floors are designed and dedicated to them. The top floor, which also serves as an observation deck, contains a representation of the interior of King Solomon's Temple and Solomon's throne room, presented by the Tall Cedars of Lebanon. The York Rite's Knights Templar sponsor a medieval chapel. The other two York Rite groups, the Royal Arch Masons and the Cryptic

The bronze statue of George Washington in Memorial Hall at the George Washington Masonic Memorial.

The 1780s replica lodge room at the George Washington Masonic Memorial, featuring artifacts from the president's life as a Freemason.

Masons, present scenes from the building of the temple, the Ark of the Covenant, and the secret crypts said to have been excavated beneath the temple during the time of Enoch. The fez-wearing Shriners International have a large display area promoting their charitable works and their twenty-three children's hospitals throughout North America. Likewise, the Mystic Order of Veiled Prophets of the Enchanted Realm, better known as the Grottoes, has a floor dedicated to its social and charitable mission. Other members of the Masonic family are represented, including the National Sojourners, other York Rite bodies, and youth groups like DeMolay International.

The memorial is open to the public for tours, and concerts frequently take place in its auditorium. In 2007, it was used as a stand-in for the Smithsonian Institute in the film *National Treasure II: Book of Secrets*.

Almas Shrine Center

Another red herring in the plot of *The Lost Symbol* concerns a clue that sends the CIA flying off to Franklin Square in search of a

Masonic connection. Sure enough, there is one there, though it is only mentioned in passing. The Almas Shrine Center is located at 1315 K Street NW, on the northwest corner of Franklin Square, and it really does have a secret.

The Ancient Arabic Nobles of the Mystic Shrine, known today officially as Shriners International, is an appendant body of Free-masonry that originated in the 1870s as a high-spirited, hard-drinking alternative to the tee-totaling Masonic lodges. Even though they had started in taverns, Freemasons in the United States started tossing the booze out of their lodges in the 1840s, partially as an answer to criticism leveled at them during the strong anti-Masonic period between 1829 and about 1843. A group of Masons met in New York at the Knickerbocker Cottage and decided to form a group strictly for having fun. Led by Dr. Walter M. Fleming, M.D., and actor William J.

The Arabic-styled Almas Shrine Center in Franklin Square.

Florence, they fabricated the organization around a ritual and vocabulary based on an exaggerated imitation of Arab culture.

Almost from the beginning, Shriners, who are readily identified by their distinctive red fezzes, quickly became pegged as professional party animals. They are world-renowned as much for the little cars and marching units in which they appear in parades as for their philanthropy, along with occasionally riding their motorcycles or horses through a hotel lobby. The Shriners Hospitals comprise twenty-two hospitals across North America that provide care, at no charge to families, for children who have orthopedic problems or related diseases.

The Almas Shrine building, located in the business area of Washington, D.C., looks strangely out of place on Franklin Square with its distinctive Arabic facade. Built on the eve of the Great Depression in 1929, it could easily be mistaken for a mosque, with its pointed arches and its beautiful terra-cotta tile work. It houses offices for the Potentate and other officers of the local Shrine. It contains one of the city's most impressive ballrooms and can accommodate 400 guests, and the Sphinx Club, with its characteristic vaulted arches, is a true hidden treasure in the district. There is also an auditorium and smaller rooms where the Shrine and some of its groups hold meetings.

Famed "March King" John Philip Sousa, a member of Almas, was the honorary director of their Shrine Band until his death in 1932. He composed the march *Nobles of the Mystic Shrine* in 1923.

The biggest secret of the Almas Shrine is that it was not really built at this location. At one time, the Shrine owned the entire block now dominated by the Franklin Square office complex. In 1987, to make way for the new office building, its Arabesque facade was dismantled brick by brick into 35,000 pieces, numbered, catalogued, moved, and reassembled in its present spot. The meeting rooms, auditorium, and dining space are all new construction.

The National Cathedral

One of the most common modern notions about the Founding Fathers is that they were overwhelmingly Deistic, and there is a sense today that the First Amendment guarantee of freedom *of* religion was supposed to mean freedom *from* religion.

The L'Enfant plan for Washington, D.C., included a prominent place for a great church "intended for national purposes, such as public prayer, thanksgiving, funeral orations, etc., and assigned to the special use of no particular Sect or denomination, but equally open to all."[5] It was to be at the intersection of 8th Street and Pennsylvania Avenue, between Congress and the President's House, where both could derive spiritual inspiration from it.

The National Cathedral.

The great church of L'Enfant's plan was never constructed, at least not where he wanted it. The National Cathedral was not begun until 1907, and it took nearly a century to construct. In spite of the government support that its name might imply, it is an Episcopal church, built with private donations. Its official name is the Cathedral Church of Saint Peter and Saint Paul, and it sits on Mount Saint Alban, one of the highest spots in the northwest area of the District of Columbia.

In *The Lost Symbol*, Dan Brown claims that the Washington Monument is the highest building in the city, but because of its location, the top of the National Cathedral is technically higher than the capstone of the monument, though the Washington Monument is still the *tallest* building in the city.

Built in the Gothic style, it is the sixth-largest cathedral in the world. It has been the location for state funerals, such as Ronald Reagan's, as well as places of national mourning, such as the prayer service after the 9/11 attacks. It is every bit as impressive, majestic, and inspirational as the great cathedrals of Europe after which it is patterned, and it continues to serve the sort of purpose that L'Enfant envisioned. It has even become the final resting place for Americans as diverse as Woodrow Wilson and Helen Keller, among more than 150 others.

Outside of the cathedral, at the west entrance, is an equestrian statue showing George Washington riding his horse Man o' War to church. Inside the cathedral itself is a very different image of Washington from those usually depicted in paintings or statues, and it repres

the combination of Freemasonry and the sacred art of cathedral building.

Washington stands dressed in a long coat—his Sunday best—respectfully holding his hat in his hand. On the wall behind the president are medallions depicting symbols of Freemasonry—a gavel, a square, and a compass. The afternoon sun bathes the scene in the dazzling colors of red and blue from the stained-glass windows nearby. Sculptor Lee Lawrie was renowned for his Art Deco creations throughout the 1920s and '30s; perhaps his most famous work is the bronze Atlas holding the world over Rockefeller Center in New York. Yet when it came to the president, Lawrie said, "I have tried to show not the soldier, not the president, but the man Washington, coming into Christ Church,

George Washington sculpture by artist Lee Lawrie in the National Cathedral, placed by the Scottish Rite.

Alexandria, pausing a moment before going down the aisle to his pew."[6] The medallions on the wall behind Washington depict the Masonic square and compass and a gavel.

The National Cathedral may well be the last Gothic cathedral ever built in the world using the medieval styles and forms. No steel was used to reinforce it, and nothing was mass-produced. While visiting the cathedral, ask about the many gargoyles and grotesques that adorn its arches, spires, and crevasses. (In case you wondered, a gargoyle carries water away from the building with a channel or pipe running through its mouth, while a grotesque deflects water by bouncing it from its head, nose, or other bulbous protuberances.) There are cats and dogs, a little girl with pigtails, and the usual array of bizarre Gothic creatures. There's even a fat politician, chomping a cigar and stuffing cash into his pockets. Try to spot the malevolent grotesque of the

The "Space Window" in the Warren Bay of the National Cathedral contains a moon rock, commemorating the Apollo 11 mission.

Dark Lord of the Sith, Darth Vader. Just as Dan Brown said, while it is admittedly a bizarre addition to a Christian house of worship, it was placed there as part of a children's contest. Don't worry, it's not close to the altar—you'll need your binoculars.

The Library of Congress

One last stop on Dan Brown's Washington, D.C., tour map. In *The Lost Symbol*, Robert Langdon and Katherine Solomon escape the authorities by riding out of the Jefferson Building of the Library of Congress on an underground conveyor belt that runs underneath 2nd Street NE to the John Adams Building. The conveyor belt that Langdon and Katherine escape on is real.

The Library of Congress was created in 1800 when the government officially moved from Philadelphia to the new city of Washing-

The Reading Room of the Jefferson Building of the Library of Congress.

ton. Congress authorized funds for a library containing "such books as may be necessary for the use of Congress—and for putting up a suitable apartment for containing them therein . . ." Of course, the massive three-building complex of the Library of Congress is a little more elaborate today than a "suitable apartment."

The original library was housed in a room in the new Capitol building until August 1814, when invading British troops marched through the city, burning or otherwise busting up everything in sight. The small library went up in flames.

A month later, former President Thomas Jefferson offered his personal library of 6,487 books as a replacement. From that new beginning, the collection today has grown to more than 130 million items, including more than 29 million cataloged books and other print materials, in 460 languages.

In 1886, following disagreements and design contests, Congress approved a new Beaux Arts Library building designed by Washington architects John L. Smithmeyer and Paul J. Pelz. The new Library of Congress building opened on November 1, 1897, and was touted as the "largest, costliest, and safest" library building in the world. Safety was a real concern in days when gas lights and paper books made for a flammable combination.

More than forty American painters and sculptors were commissioned to create works that filled every inch of wall and ceiling space. The building itself is a work of art, and you can spend hours craning your neck to study the paintings, frescoes, personal seals, names, faces, and quotations of the greatest minds and achievements of the last 3,000 years, interspersed with gods, goddesses, and even cherubs depicted using modern inventions like the telephone. Throughout the library, there are many different depictions of Minerva, the goddess of wisdom, peace, and reason, including a beautiful mosaic at the top of the staircase leading to the observation deck overlooking the Reading Room.[7]

The Jefferson Building is really in two parts. The Great Hall is the area commonly toured by the public and includes paintings and murals. The upper floor contains the North Gallery, used for exhibits, and the South Gallery, for Thomas Jefferson's original personal library.

The Main Reading Room, with its distinctive domed ceiling and desks arranged in circle, is open to researchers. It was depicted in scenes in the 2007 film *National Treasure: Book of Secrets*.

There is also a private reading room reserved for members of Congress, which can only be visited by the taxpayer by special permission. On the ceiling of that room are seven round ceiling panels. The artist, Carl Gutherz. took the colors of the spectrum that go together to make up white light and painted each panel in a different hue—red, orange, yellow,

Mosaic of Minerva in the Library of Congress.

green, blue, indigo, and violet. The panels also depict the spectrum of intelligence and achievement: faith in God; excellence through progress; truth destroying ignorance; learning through research; science harnessing nature; literature and poetry; and, finally, liberty, suffrage, justice, and equality placed in the care of the state. The symbols are there to inspire those who govern us, make our laws, and affect our lives every day, whether they have ever bothered to gaze up at them over their copies of Roll Call or not.

CHAPTER 9

Noetics

◙☒◻>ⲅ∟∨

What hath God wrought?
NUMBERS 23:23

This was the first message sent in 1844 by inventor Samuel Morse when he demonstrated the telegraph to members of Congress in the U.S. Capitol building. The message ushered in the age of instant communication and was a metaphorical melding of science with religion.

Running through a lot of the philosophical discussions in *The Lost Symbol* is the thread of a very basic human dilemma, namely, that intelligent people are also people without faith. In Brown's view, no scientist (and apparently, no symbologist) who is a product of reason and technology could look you straight in the eye and tell you he believes in a rational higher power. As in many of the metaphysical tug-of-wars that are played out in Brown's books, various characters are mouthpieces for various points of view. And, like his other books, *The Lost Symbol* suggests that he has uncovered the solution to this Question of the Ages in the science of quantum physics.

Give credit where it's due: Dan Brown's novels always manage to take on far bigger issues than your average "Who's got the microfilm?" thriller. As in Brown's other books, the action-packed chase scenes in *The Lost Symbol* are frequently punctuated with theological debates and ruminations on the nature of mankind. This time, he attempts to reconcile the struggle between science and faith by exploring a field few had ever heard of before: noetics.

Noetic science was not invented by Brown for his novel, although the description of a noetics lab within the Smithsonian's very real support center in Maryland is a complete fabrication. To fully grasp what the emerging field of noetics is and is not, it's important to look at some of the ancient and modern science behind it, and the central question of science versus faith that all of the characters in *The Lost Symbol* seem to be obsessed with.

Brown's book circles around one of the oldest ideas in Western civilization, an idea that was intensely debated by many of the great Enlightenment philosophers of the eighteenth century—that science and faith are two separate, utterly irreconcilable forces. In other words, choose sides, partner; you're either one of us or one of them. The startling scientific developments of the last fifty years have only brought this idea into sharper focus; test-tube babies, DNA, particle colliders, alcoholics growing themselves a new liver in a Petri dish— it's all a little scary sometimes for those with an old-fashioned point of view. People often see scientists and the faithful as our ancestors saw the Yankees and the Confederates: two separate camps, armed to the teeth, in constant opposition.

For some who embrace science, religion is indeed what Marx called "the opiate of the masses," a world in which Bible-thumping rogues mislead the desperate and the ignorant to achieve their own dark ends.

For some of the faithful, those who revere science are without conscience, viewing the humanity they supposedly serve as if it were a teeming mass of spores under a microscope, and making themselves gods in their ruthless pursuit of knowledge that by rights belongs to the Creator alone.

Yet, despite the persistence of these attitudes, history tells us that through the centuries, for educated people of both camps, science and religion have not been in constant and polar opposition. In the past couple of decades, long and scholarly articles have been written, even for popular news magazines, putting forward the "surprising" notion that the two are closer than people think. The fact is that this isn't a new idea at all. Science and faith are not irreconcilable, and what's more, they never have been.

Isaac Newton and Albert Einstein, the two great pillars upon which modern physics has been built, were both men of faith.

Newton was the proverbial mad genius, and his contributions to the "new science" were remarkable: As a mathematician, he proved the theory of gravity and created the discipline of calculus; his groundbreaking work on optics uncovered the very nature of light refraction, and he built the first reflective telescope; in his *Principia* he established the basic laws of physics that ruled both our own

Sir Isaac Newton: "This most beautiful system could only proceed from the dominion of an intelligent and powerful Being."

planet and the orbital dynamics of astronomy. But definitely, he was a man of faith; one of his passions during his long life was his Kabbalistic, mathematical study of secret codes in biblical prophecy, particularly in Daniel and the Book of Revelation.

As for Albert Einstein, the scientific giant straddling the twentieth century, he always conceded that religion was an important part of a society's ethical framework. In later years, Einstein wrote a great deal on the subject of religion versus science, and his ideas would fit right in with New Age thinking. He believed in a nonpersonal God who designed with perfection the clockwork mechanism of the universe. His was the quest of a man of faith to discover the workings of that universe. This was very much in tune with the philosophy of Deism (the notion that God created the universe and set it in motion, but is not involved in our personal lives) that influenced so many of our Founding Fathers.

However, though he didn't think much of formal religion, Einstein did describe himself as a "deeply religious man." In one of his most famous statements, he succinctly summed up the idea that science and faith are not only reconcilable but interconnected: "Science without religion is lame, religion without science is blind."

Nowhere is this issue of the wedding of the heart and the head more in evidence than in the relatively new science of quantum physics and its extension in one of the books that inspired Dan Brown to write about "noetic science": Lynne McTaggart's *The Intention Experiment*. McTaggart is not a scientist, which is why her exciting book can be understood by anyone. Like the gentleman of the old school that he is, Brown gives full credit to McTaggart on page 56 of *The Lost Symbol*, citing her work as the inspiration for the fictional character of Katherine Solomon. Being a gracious lady of the old school, McTaggart has expressed her appreciation to Brown for helping her important book reach a much wider audience (rather than suing him, as Michael Baigent and Richard Leigh did when Brown gave credit to their book, *Holy Blood, Holy Grail* in the text of *The Da Vinci Code*).

McTaggart's previous book, *The Force*, covered much of the same ground, but more from a medical perspective of healing through the power of thought or prayer. The character of Katherine Solomon is given a lab at the Smithsonian by her brother, Peter Solomon, so that she can pursue experiments in this exciting new field, a field based around the concept that human thoughts, in an alpha state of deep concentration, have the power to affect matter and living things.

> Katherine's work here had begun using modern science to answer ancient philosophical questions. *Does anyone hear our prayers? Is there life after death? Do humans have souls?* Incredibly, Katherine had answered all of these questions, and more. Scientifically. Conclusively.
>
> *The Lost Symbol*, page 208

There really *is* a Katherine Solomon. Her name is Marilyn Schlitz, and she is the real-life president of the Institute of Noetic Sciences in Petaluma, California. In an interview with National Public Radio, Schlitz said she could identify ten experiments carried out by the

Institute in *The Lost Symbol.* While she doesn't resemble Dan Brown's description physically, there are other similarities. Schlitz's father and brother were 32° Scottish Rite Freemasons. Like the fictional character, Schlitz started her career at nineteen, studying prayer and healing, distant intention, and ancient mystery traditions.

Apollo 14 Astronaut Edgar Mitchell, founder of the Institute of Noetic Science.

And like Katherine Solomon, Schlitz believes ancient wisdom traditions predicted modern scientific discoveries.[1]

The Institute of Noetic Science was founded in 1973 by Apollo 14 astronaut Ed Mitchell and industrialist Paul N. Temple. Mitchell claimed to have an epiphany during the three-day flight back to Earth from the moon.

> The biggest joy was on the way home. In my cockpit window every 2 minutes I saw the earth, the moon, the sun and the whole 360 degree panorama of the heavens. It was a powerful overwhelming experience. Suddenly, I realized the molecules of my body and the molecules of the spacecraft and the molecules in the bodies of my partners were prototyped and manufactured in some ancient generation of stars. It was an overwhelming sense of oneness, a connectedness. . . . The presence of divinity became almost palpable, and I knew that life in the universe was not just an accident based on random processes.[2]

To understand *The Lost Symbol,* it helps to understand some basic concepts of physics. So, for the uninitiated, and those who flunked physics in high school, let's all start with a few simple definitions: First, what is physics, and second, what is quantum physics?

"Physics" simply means the study of the natural world in all its forms; in many respects, it's just another word for science. It comes from the Latin word *physica*, meaning the natural sciences. Three centuries ago, this included the science of medicine, hence the word physician. This youthful science of physics sounds simple enough to the modern mind; it's merely the science of matter, and how and why matter reacts to a variety of forces. Sounds pretty easy.

But the discipline of physics most commonly heard of by non-scientists is the physics of radiation and the atom. The existence of atoms—particles of matter too small to be seen by the naked eye—had been proposed for some time, in fact, as far back as the Greek philosophers Leucippus and Democritus in the fifth century B.C. and Epicurus in the fourth century B.C. All of these men studied the same intriguing issues of motion, the mathematical formulas of action and reaction, and the nature of the physical world. These issues were also dissected by geniuses of the ancient world like Aristotle and Archimedes.

During Europe's Dark Ages, these works on physics by the Greek masters were cherished and protected by the great Islamic universities in Spain in the seventeenth century. And when Islamic learning entered its own dark age, brought on by a new wave of Islamic fundamentalism, the Renaissance men of science in the West were able to rediscover these works.

But still, insofar as atoms were concerned, it was all just theory, angels on pinheads, as it were. It wasn't until the early 1900s that scientists began to accept the truth of the existence of atoms.

The great rebirth of science in the West would produce the great minds that moved mechanical physics forward: Copernicus, Kepler, Galileo, Descartes, and at last the crowning glory of Isaac Newton.

Mankind was indeed moving in the right direction, but around 1896, science erupted, lurching forward at the speed of a rocket. In that year radium was isolated, and radioactivity was discovered. In 1905 Einstein gave the world the theory of relativity, propelling mathematics into the twentieth century, and proving the existence of molecular matter at the atomic level even before the invention of ion microscopes that could actually see atoms.

And then came quantum physics.

> The great irony is that all the religions of the world, for cen-
> turies, have been urging their followers to embrace the concept
> of faith and belief . . . the power of focused conviction and inten-
> tion. The same science that eroded our faith in the miraculous is
> now building a bridge back across the chasm it created.[3]

This was the next big change, our journey from the molecular world to the atomic world and, finally, the subatomic. It's important to note that the whole idea of quantum physics, the behavior of particles smaller than the atom, was born in the mind of Albert Einstein in the 1920s. Later, he decided he had been wrong. In the meanwhile, several other scientists all over the world, the most famous being Niels Bohr, had already taken up the idea and run with it, doing quantum research of their own. Bohr and his colleagues most emphatically did not agree with Einstein that his quantum theories had been wrong. In fact, the two men had a lively, twenty-year debate on the subject. The battle was on over the shape and substance of reality.

With Einstein in the lead, physicists proved that the nucleus of the atom is made up of protons, neutrons, and electrons, all held together by a nuclear force. If this force could be broken, the positively charged protons would fly apart, violently. With this knowledge, physicists like Einstein, Enrico Fermi, and Robert Oppenheimer loaded the weight of the atom bomb onto the world's shoulders.

But a great deal of good came out of physics as well, including subatomic quantum physics, which has revealed exciting wonders, many of which are only now beginning to be understood, that may benefit humanity.

Simply put, early in the twentieth century, classical physicists thought that "wave" atoms, like light, behaved one way, and "particle" atoms behaved in another way. But quantum physics went deeper than the atom, to the much smaller subatomic particles, and in the process discovered that they didn't play by the rules. These particles could have both wave and particle characteristics at the same time.

Einstein's idea of determinism and solidity in the universe was dying. Quantum physics eventually proved, in what's known as "the Heisenberg uncertainty principle," that to accurately determine in any given moment both the position and speed of particles this small is impossible. Subatomic particles are not stable, and what's even more difficult to grasp, they're not exactly in a state of being. This exciting new principle was the brainchild of Werner Heisenberg, who, together with the founding father of quantum physics, Bohr, called the second half of their joint theory the Copenhagen Interpretation, which is their explanation for the uncertainty principle. They concluded that subatomic particles exist in a state of potentiality; everything is probability and outcome. A particle doesn't really exist standing alone; instead, it only exists in relation to other particles. As Lynne McTaggart explains, it is ". . . not like a little solar system of billiard balls but something far more messy; tiny clouds of probability."[4]

And they also have some very funky little quirks that sends quantum physics into the realm of philosophy as much as science. Because once these subatomic particles have been in contact with one another, they continue to influence one another, to actually *react* to one another, as if with a magnetic force, even after they are separated. They pass energy back and forth to one another, as if to imply that the entirety of the universe's mass and energy is related in a mesh that can't truly be broken. The universe, as McTaggart so elegantly describes it, is "not a storehouse of static, separate objects, but a single organism of interconnected energy fields in a continuous state of becoming."[5]

And as if this isn't tough enough to get your brain around, there's the corollary phenomenon that in experiments these subatomic particles of probability would collapse into a solid particle only when scientists attempted to measure them. Then, they became something in a particular state. In other words, they were actually affected by observation.

To put it more bluntly, "reality" is not immutable; it's determined, not by rock-solid existence, but by the observer. What you see and do is shaped by the fact that you're seeing it and doing it. Though it seems astonishing to even contemplate, it appears that the energy of human consciousness is a part of this web of subatomic probability, that thoughts are *things*, parcels of subatomic reality that may be able to influence other reality.

In a few corners of the world, some brave scientists (you can always tell the pioneers by the arrows in their backs) began to experiment with this notion of "psychokinesis," or the power of intention contained within human consciousness while in an alpha state of meditation or prayer. McTaggart's catalog of experiments being done in this area so far are nothing less than staggering in their potential implications. *The Intention Experiment* ends, interestingly enough, by inviting the reader to participate in experiments in mass thought projections put together on the Web.

While a deep explanation of the subtle complexities of quantum physics is beyond the scope of this book, an excellent place to start if you know nothing of the subject is *The Quantum World, Quantum Physics for Everyone*, by Kenneth W. Ford.

Of course, Lynne McTaggart rightly refers to intention theory as a pioneer science, but this doesn't stop Dan Brown from going a bit far with it; sometimes he makes quantum physics and noetic theory sound like one of Clark Kent's superpowers—the ability to use thoughts in a supercosmic, *Bewitched* fashion, as if we have within easy reach the means to think hard enough to start the car on a snowy morning without having to go outside. Near the end of the novel, both Solomons, brother and sister, compare noetics to the "Ancient Mysteries," which reads like a sort of Brownian chop suey of the Hindu Vedas, the Kabbalistic Zohar, biblical prophecy, Buddhism, and just about any other occult or self-empowerment guidebook, including the collected works of Dale Carnegie.

Doubtless, after the number Brown did on the Catholic Church in *The Da Vinci Code*, there were lots of readers out there who were shocked to find that the MacGuffin propelling *The Lost Symbol* is a gory search for the Lost Word of Masonic ritual, which turns out to be *the* Word, the Bible, a sacred book to Freemasons.

Parenthetically, this seems as good a place as any to point out, however, that the holy book on the altar in a Masonic lodge is not necessarily the Bible, though the Bible is doubtless the most popular text. The holy book on the altar is whatever is most sacred to the majority of men in that particular lodge; it could be the Jewish Tanakh, the Hindu Upanishads or the Buddhist Dhammapada. To give comfort to members of a very diverse lodge, there may be two holy books on the altar, and in some cases, even as many as three. For example, in Israel many lodges place a Bible, a Torah, and a Qu'ran side by side on the altar.

So, for any of you who may fear that Dan Brown has gone the way of Anne Rice and become an evangelical Christian, the answer to that is, it's not likely. Though the Bible turns out to be the Lost Word everyone is chasing, Brown describes it as being part of a larger whole, the collected knowledge of the "Ancient Mysteries."

Old Warner Brothers cartoons can be enjoyed on two levels; the kids are laughing at the antics of Bugs Bunny chasing Elmer Fudd around with a razor, while the adults are laughing just as loudly at the beautifully orchestrated spoof of a Rossini opera. In the closing chapters of *The Lost Symbol*, Peter Solomon states that the same is true of the Bible, that it contains simple stories and ethical parables for the kids and all the lowbrows, along with secret messages of the ancients hidden inside them for those bright enough to find them.

It's a snooty, Ivy League version of Jewish Kabbalism, the endless search for secret, encoded messages and prophecies within the Old Testament of the Bible. But, according to Peter Solomon, that undiscovered secret of the Bible, that "lost word," is that God is within us all, literally, not metaphorically. We have the power in our minds to have our own apotheosis, to find the god that exists inside us and links us to the ethereal goo of the minds of the rest of humanity. In other words, that heaving mass of chaotic thought is god.

In the final scenes of the book, during which Katherine and Robert are high above the floor of the Capitol rotunda examining the fresco *The Apotheosis of Washington* by Constantino Brumidi, a lively exchange of ideas on this subject of the mind as god goes on, in the sort of Saturday night dorm-room conversations that Brown specializes in.

In this final scene, for Katherine and Robert, the word "apotheosis" means, in its most simplistic terms, the raising of a man into a god. But on a subtler level, for a painter, it means an angelic glorification of a dead subject. The artist Brumidi was half-Greek and half-Roman. Greeks loved apotheosis imagery even more than Italians. With their long-standing history of belief that great men were related to or became gods, the suggestion of an apotheosis in a painting came to be a common metaphor for a man of greatness, implying not so much that he had literally become a god but that he had been carried up on clouds of glory to the pantheon of the great, above the reach of ordinary men.

In the Brownian context, then, Brumidi's famous fresco is there to guide the lawmakers below and the nation as well in a sort of New Age quest to become god by finding the god within ourselves, just as the authors of the Ancient Mysteries have tried to hammer into our thick heads for centuries.

Okay. If you like.

For Brown, this apotheosis is not metaphorical but quite real—the ultimate deification of the "Me Generation."

Personally, I prefer the idea that there is actually a force out there that's a little larger than the trinity of me, myself, and I. They say only fools argue about the existence of God, since neither side can ever hope to offer up any solid, empirical evidence; it's all anecdotal, based on what's happened to you that's made you believe as you do.

But then again, maybe the twenty-first century isn't all science and no faith, after all. In the last couple of decades, humanity's attempts to build a so-called particle collider that would slam protons together in a miles-long underground facility and create something theoretical called the Higgs bosun particle, hasn't met with much success. The idea is to help us understand how mass in the universe was created by creating that mass ourselves. Each time the collision occurred would be like a little "Big Bang" of the creation-of-the-universe theory. In other words, all these white-coated Dr. Frankensteins don't want to study matter, or understand matter, or even use matter; they want to *create* matter. Supposedly it would take mankind leaps ahead in our understanding of matter and where it comes from. Even more tantalizing, if one accepts the popular "string theory"—an incredibly complex quantum theory that's all Greek to most mortals—we could, in theory at least, discover other dimensions of existence unknown to us.

The American government was going to build a particle-collider in Texas, but the idea was never popular. There were all sorts of fears that forcibly colliding these subatomic particles that are already traveling near the speed of light could have absolutely biblical consequences, from blowing the Earth off the cosmic map to creating a black hole that would swallow us up. Besides, since the multinational researchers at CERN (in French, this is an acronym for the European Council for Nuclear Research) were already building a huge facility outside of Geneva, it was decided to drop the Texas project and save a few billion.

The project has been plagued by problems over the last few years; mysterious breakdowns, explosions, and in 2009, a project scientist arrested for alleged links to the terrorist group al-Qaeda. At this point, a lot of the scientists on the project, people who are supposedly without faith, reportedly have begun to wonder if the hand of something larger is stopping them from successfully pulling off this feat.

At first, these remarks were only Internet rumors. But a 2009 article in the *London Times* came right out and stated that there were shredded nerves coming unglued all over Geneva. The Large Hadron Collider, or LHC, might just be under a state of metaphysical siege. And this isn't coming from the crackpot element; several heavy-hitter physicists from the Niels Bohr Institute and the Yukawa Institute in Japan are putting forward some hair-raising ideas. They believe it may be possible, proved through their mathematical formulae, that these setbacks are coming from the future, with either man or machine twisting time in order to stop the LHC from ever fulfilling its mission, a mission which could be "abhorrent to nature."

To put it even more bluntly, Holger Bech Nielsen of the Niels Bohr Institute stated, "You could explain it by saying that God rather hates Higgs bosun particles and attempts to avoid them."[6]

And so, a note for Mr. Brown: being able to think hard enough to bend a spoon without touching it is indeed a remarkable thing, but it may not be enough to qualify you to enter into a state of godhood. *Laus Deo*.

CHAPTER 10

Whence Come You, and Whither Are You Traveling?

∀◻◻◦L◻ L◦⊐◻ <ᴄ<, ⊐◦⊐
'◻ᴦ>◻◻ᴦ ⊐ᴦ◻ <ᴄ< >ᴦ⅃∧◦ᴸᴦ◻⊓

> It is the glory of God to conceal a thing
> PROVERBS 25:2, *KING JAMES VERSION OF THE BIBLE*

> It is the glory of God to conceal the word
> PROVERBS 25:2, *DOUAY-RHEIMS BIBLE*

Dan Brown's *The Lost Symbol* is first, last, and always, a work of fiction, if not downright fantasy. If there was any question, one need only be reminded that all through the book he describes the Washington Redskins making it into the NFC playoffs. Like any novelist, he doesn't let reality get in the way of a good story.

Star Trek creator Gene Roddenberry was once asked, since every time the U.S.S. *Enterprise* was hit by an enemy attack the ship would roll to one side and the whole crew would fall out of their seats, why didn't the show's art department just add seat belts to the chairs on the bridge? Roddenberry replied, "Because then they couldn't fall out of their seats."

Dan Brown writes high-speed, action-packed thrillers that are wrapped around a game of Trivial Pursuit™, and his fans forgive him even the biggest whoppers. So, they don't bother to ask why the CIA is handling a domestic kidnapping case when in reality the FBI and the U.S. Park Police would be the bungling plodders investigating and chasing Langdon around town in helicopters. And it doesn't bother them a bit that a hydrogen explosion at least the size of the Hindenburg doesn't result in half the city being evacuated. Or even that Peter Solomon would let his sister and friend die rather than tell Mal'akh what the Lost Word really is because he isn't a Mason but then goes ahead and tells Robert Langdon in the end. As Roddenberry said, if he fixed all that stuff, then they couldn't fall out of their seats.

Yet, Dan Brown has spawned a vast countryside of critics eager to tell some 50 or 60 million of his fans just where he went wrong. Perhaps our mothers were right when they told us the bullies were beating us to a pulp and stealing our milk money "because they're just jealous, honey."

Brown's toughest critics are the philosophical ones. They will forgive him for using too many italics and putting Washington neighborhoods in the wrong part of town. What bothers them are the bigger ideas.

Early in the book, Robert Langdon is teaching his Harvard class and asks them: "What are the three prerequisites for an ideology to be considered a religion?" The answers a student gives are, "Assure, Believe, Convert," which are explained as meaning to *assure* salvation, *believe* in a precise theology, and *convert* nonbelievers.[1]

Well, that's certainly one form of religion, and there's no dearth of religious groups that believe strongly in conversion of nonbelievers. Catholics, Baptists, Mormons, Pentecostals, Muslims, and even Scientologists would agree. But Jews certainly have no doctrine that compels them to convert non-Jews. Neither do Hindus, Buddhists, or most other Eastern religions. There has long been a debate in this country between historians and theologians over whether America was founded as a Christian nation or not. The fact that the argument still rages on suggests there is enough uncertainty over the matter to keep quarrelling about it.

What is certain is that the United States was not formed in 1776 and chartered by its Constitution in September of 1787 as a Puritan, or Episcopalian, or Catholic, or Lutheran, or Jewish nation. The colonies themselves had been settled over the previous century by pockets of religious groups who stuck together: Quakers in Pennsylvania, Congregationalists on Long Island, Lutherans in Delaware, Catholics in Maryland, Presbyterians in New Jersey, and so on. Immigrants coming to America seeking to practice their own brand of God-bothering without being bothered in return by intolerant neighbors had to learn the hard lesson of becoming tolerant themselves.

Freemasonry developed at this exact moment in time and made religious and political tolerance, at least within the walls of its lodges, an unbreakable rule. The Masons wrote this tolerance into their original laws, or Constitutions. And the men who became Masons saw how such a system could work, not by disagreeing but by finding the common beliefs they all shared. To the Founding Fathers who were also Freemasons, these ideas became the bedrock of their designs for the country.

What often gets left out of the discussion of both the Enlightenment and Freemasonry is that the most admirable historical figures who were scientists, mathematicians, economists, and philosophers were also deeply religious people. Just because they read their Bible regularly and sat in a pew on Sunday did not mean they checked their ability to reason and innovate in the cloakroom. And just because they developed reasoned, rational thoughts on the most vexing subjects of their age did not mean that a strong belief in God got pitched out the window with the bath water as silly superstition. Faith and reason are not mutually exclusive terms, and favoring one path over another is not necessarily a suicide pact.

In *The Lost Symbol*, Peter Solomon claims the Bible is a Gnostic document that the unworthy cannot understand without being properly instructed in the Ancient Mysteries.[2] Brown seems to imply that the Bible is itself a coded message that requires some secret, lost knowledge before it can be correctly interpreted. In particular, Revelation is presented as a mysterious, unfathomable work that the average unlearned boob can't possibly comprehend. I'll grant you that Revelation is a tough nut to crack. But Brown himself makes the same mistake as his own character Mal'akh does in thinking that the "Ancient Mysteries" are some magic key that will unlock the secrets of the universe, and that those who came before us were far more cunning, wise, and gifted than we could ever possibly be. It's sort of a philosophical version of sitting in a rocker on the porch and muttering to the grandkids, "It's just not like the good old days."

> And the serpent said unto the woman, Ye shall not surely die: For God doth know that in the day ye eat thereof, then your eyes shall be opened, and ye shall be as gods, knowing good and evil."
>
> Genesis 3:4–5

This is the taunt of Eden's serpent. "Ye shall become as gods" is Brown's way of twisting the words to suit his own meaning by cherrypicking from the quote. Brown's version is that intellect is the same as religion. And it seems that if modern science, government, and social reconstruction theories like socialism and communism proclaim "There is no God," that means there's a vacancy to be filled on the cloud behind the pearly gates by the really, *really* smart people, who "shall be as gods." Brown seems to imply that the Freemasons hold the inside straight in this game.

However, Freemasonry has never advanced that as its message. Masonry taught its members from its beginning that faith is the private business between a man and God, whatever he perceives God to be. The lodge does not practice a religion; it has no plan for salvation; it hopes for (but does not promise) an afterlife. Likewise, politics is forbidden as a topic of conversation in the lodge.

Certainly there were eighteenth-century French *philosophes* and English Enlightenment thinkers in their private rooms who propounded those kinds of notions. Once they successfully hurled kings who claimed divine privilege from their thrones, chucked the clergy out of their monasteries over their tax bills, and completely rewrote the rules of government, the Enlightenment "reformers" undoubtedly felt buffed up with the steroids of egotism and invincibility. Becoming "as gods" would be a logical next step, which was why papal bulls and encyclicals were flung down from the Vatican for 150 years about the dangerous ideas being propounded by "free thinkers." Men like the Founding Fathers were among the most perilous people on the planet to those who depended upon the status quo.

The *Laus Deo* motto on the capstone of the Washington Monument means what it says: "Praise God." It wasn't stuck up there to show man's (or Freemasonry's) triumph over the elements and elevation to the front porch of heaven. It is an exhortation for every man to look to the sky, to praise God as the Grand Architect of the Universe.

On the other hand, given the stormy history of the monument's construction, it might just have been one massive, collective sigh of relief that the darned thing was finally finished.

The Lost Word

In one of the ritual ceremonies of Freemasonry, the blindfolded candidate approaches the Master of the Lodge, who asks him, "From whence come you, and whither are you traveling?" The Senior Deacon, who is conducting him through the ceremony answers for him:

> *From the West and traveling to the East.*
> *Of what are you in pursuit?*
> *That which was lost, which by my endeavors and your assistance, I am in hopes to find.*[3]

The lifelong symbolic quest of the Freemason is the search for self-knowledge, the quest for truth—the Lost Word. It is a mission that can never come to a successful conclusion, at least until the dirt is thrown over our heads. Robert Langdon's nemesis in *The Lost Symbol*, Mal'akh, doesn't understand this simple lesson, believing the Lost Word is a real, tangible word or symbol that, once tattooed on the top of his head in blood with a crow's feather, will give him the secret knowledge of all time and raise him to a new stage of invincibility. He discovers, too late, that he has been chasing a chimera.

Zachary Solomon transforms himself into Mal'akh and follows the Aleister Crowley path: "Make yourself sacred." He chases the abracadabra side of "magickal" thought, looking for a secret word that will change him. He believes the Lost Word of Freemasonry really is a word, a talisman, an incantation. In Chapter 4, I discussed the *ouroboros*, the image of the snake eating its own tail. In ancient and medieval times, the ouroboros was a symbol of life, death, and rebirth, or as Dan Brown expresses it, "at one ment." However, the snake eating itself may ultimately be an allegory of the obsessive esoteric alchemist, who ceaselessly chases his own tail in search of some special, occult knowledge that doesn't really exist. As Langdon says,

> "[Mal'akh]'s made the same error many zealots make—confusing metaphor with literal reality." Similarly, early alchemists had toiled in vain to transform lead into gold, never realizing that lead-to-gold was nothing but a metaphor for tapping into true human potential—that of taking a dull, ignorant mind and transforming it into a bright, enlightened one.
>
> *The Lost Symbol*, page 80

The Freemasons who formed the fraternity in the early 1700s in Scotland and England were Enlightenment-era thinkers. They believed in science and reason, not magic, hocus pocus, and alchemical dabblings. They fought against superstition. In continental Europe, Rosicrucians and lovers of mysticism introduced occult, hermetic, and Kabbalistic references into what became the "higher" degrees of the Scottish Rite in the early nineteenth century. That doesn't make them bad or wrong or misguided, or even inauthentic Masons. But it marked a strong philosophical divergence in Freemasonry that exists even today.

Masonic author Rex Hutchens, in his 2006 introduction to Albert Pike's *Lecture on Masonic Symbolism*, wrote,

> The scholars of the eighteenth and nineteenth centuries, alive with a newfound intellectual freedom, sought everything everywhere, and often found it—or thought they did. Rank speculation stood beside precise scholarship and demanded equal sta-

tion. Too often, Pike complied. This lack of a critical faculty is clearly seen in [his book] *Morals and Dogma* and his subsequent lectures. Mixed with the erudition of Francis Bacon and the lyrical beauty of the *King James Bible* was the carping inanity of Eliphas Lévi, the witless speculations and reveries of Godfrey Higgins and Thomas Maurice.[4]

In an interview on NBC's *Dateline*, Dan Brown had an exchange with reporter Matt Lauer in which the discussion turned to the notion that modern Freemasonry has lost its way, and that, with the exception of a few pockets of enthusiastic Masons seeking greater philosophical truths in alchemical and obscure Kabbalist texts, the rest of the fraternity has become little more than fish fries and bake sales promoting their charities. That dismissive view leaves out the vast majority of Masons and lodges that fall in between those two simplistic extremes.

Interestingly, back in 1921, the noted Masonic author H. L. Haywood wrote in his essay, *A Bird's Eye View of Masonic History*:

> Freemasons, for some reason or other, always have been, and even now remain, peculiarly susceptible to the appeal of the occult; we have had some experience in this country during recent years that prove this. No doubt a learned dustman can find particles of gold buried away in the debris of occultism and the true gold, even in small quantities, is not to be despised; but the dangers attendant upon trifling with the magical are a heavy price to pay for what little we can gain. Those who have, with worn fingers, untangled the snarl of occult symbolism, tell us that these secret cults have been teaching the doctrine of the one God, of the brotherhood of man, and of the future life of the soul; all this is good but one doesn't need to wade through jungles of weird speculations in order to come upon the teachings that one may find in any Sunday School. It behooves the wise student to walk warily; perhaps the wisest things is to leave occultism altogether alone. Life is too short to tramp around its endless labyrinths. Moreover, there is on the surface of Freemasonry enough truth to equip any of us for all time to come.[5]

In reality, Freemasonry has always adapted to suit the needs of the society in which it resides, balancing esoteric thought on one side, and the needs of men to be sociable on the other. Sometimes the scales tip one way and sometimes the other way. The Freemasonry of London in 1717 was very different from Freemasonry in Paris in 1796, New York in 1843, Des Moines in 1952, and Los Angeles today. Also, let's not forget that Dan Brown is not a Mason, at least he wasn't when he wrote *The Lost Symbol*, and he seems to have taken the Romantic Age Masonic authors at face value. Anyone who claims there has been some magical, mystical Golden Age of forgotten wisdom that Masonry has strayed from today is talking out of his wizard's hat.

As I said in Chapter 3, the secret message written in Masonic cipher code on the back cover of *The Lost Symbol* reads, "All great truths begin as blasphemies." When I discovered that its source was George Bernard Shaw's play, *Annajanska, the Bolshevik Empress*, written in 1919, I looked up the context of the line. The Grand Duchess in Russia knows that the Russian Revolution means the end of her family's reign, and she is talking with a general about their impending fate:

> THE GRAND DUCHESS. Do not deceive yourself, General: never again will a Panjandrum reign in Beotia. . . . We are so decayed, so out of date, so feeble, so wicked in our own despite, that we have come at last to will our own destruction.
> GEN. STRAMMFEST. You are uttering blasphemy.
> THE GRAND DUCHESS. All great truths begin as blasphemies. All the king's horses and all the king's men cannot set up my father's throne again. If they could, you would have done it, would you not?

Given that the quote is presented in Masonic code, it is possible that Brown is sending a message to the Masons themselves that maybe Freemasonry as it is practiced today is so out of date, so feeble, so lost, that it has come to will its own destruction. Or perhaps it is a caution to the fraternity not to let such a thing happen.

I believe just the opposite will happen, in part because of *The Lost Symbol*. Through the book, Freemasonry has been introduced by

Before entering the Temple Room of the House of the Temple,
everyone must pass this marble chair with the simple warning that legend
has it was uttered by ancient Greece's Oracle of Delphi: "Know Thyself."

Dan Brown to millions of people who had either never heard of it or
had forgotten about it. Maybe he made it out to be spookier or more
high-minded than the local lodge on the corner may seem, but
Freemasonry isn't out of date, or feeble, or lost, and it is not headed
for the tar pits of history. The truth is that Freemasonry is in the midst
of remaking itself again, to serve a new generation of men in need of
its lessons, its knowledge, its tolerance, and its brotherhood that cross-
es all boundaries.

Dan Brown has another word for it.

Hope.

Endnotes

□□•□⊐□℮⊏>□∨

INTRODUCTION

1. Mark Hayward, "From 'Da Vinci' to Masons," *The Union Leader*, May 19, 2004.

2. Bill Donahue, "Dan Brown Adores the Masons," Catholic League website, September 15, 2009, http://www.catholicleague.org/release.php?id=1673 (accessed 9/17/2009).

3. BBC, *"Can we trust Dan Brown on the Freemasons?"* September 17, 2009, http://news.bbc.co.uk/2/hi/uk_news/magazine/8258575.stm (accessed September 17, 2009).

4. Maureen Dowd, "Capital Secrets," *New York Times Sunday Book Review*, September 30, 2009, http://www.nytimes.com/2009/10/11/books/review/Dowd-t.html (accessed October 10, 2009).

5. I. Edward Clark, *The Royal Secret* (Louisville, KY: J.P. Morton & Co., 1923), 159.

6. Wilhelmus Bogart Bryan, *A History of the National Capital from its Foundation Through the Adoption of the Organic Act, Vol. I* (New York: Macmillan, 1914), 66.

CHAPTER 1: ORIGIN OF THE FREEMASONS

1. Some French Masons claim they were organized under Charles Martel in the eighth century, predating the English guilds. Martel was the unifying general of the Francs, who kicked off the Middle Ages by booting out the invading Moors, and is generally credited with developing the beginnings of knighthood, chivalry, and feudalism. By making such a link, French Freemasons can claim more chivalric and noble origins than their scruffier, less noble English counterparts.

2. Dan Brown, *The Lost Symbol* (New York: Doubleday, 2009).

3. Email from Rex Hutchens to Christopher Hodapp on September 23, 2009.

4. There were approximately 7,360 members who were 33° Masons in the Southern Jurisdiction of the United States and 3,766 in the Northern Masonic Jurisdiction as of October 24, 2009.

5. *Freemasons Magazine and Masonic Mirror.* Vol. 1, (August 6, 1859), 97.

6. Ha'aretz News Agency, Religion News Blog, "Bomb blast at Istanbul Masonic lodge kills at least 2," March 10, 2004, http://www.religionnewsblog.com/6376 (accessed October 12, 2009).

7. Just as this book was going to press, it was announced that the requirement for judges to report their Masonic membership was being rescinded in light of a European Union Court of Human Rights decision which found a similar law in Italy to be discriminatory. Jack Straw, now Lord Chancellor and Secretary of State for Justice, announced on November 5, 2009, that he was scrapping the rule he introduced as Home Secretary in 1997. For more information, see Andrew Sparrow, "Jack Straw scraps rule saying judges must declare if they are masons," *The Guardian*, November 5, 2009, http://www.guardian.co.uk/politics/blog/2009/nov/05/jack-straw-judges-masons (Accessed November 5, 2009). For background on the original rules requiring police and the judiciary to register their Masonic membership, see Jason Bennetto and Colin Brown, "New judges and police told they must confess Masonic links," *The Independent*, November 22, 1999, http://www.independent.co.uk/news/new-judges-and-police-told-they-must-confess-masonic-links-1295380.html, (Accessed November 9, 2009). *See also* Home Affairs Committee, Third Report, *Freemasonry in the Police and the Judiciary*, June 19, 1998, http://www.charlton.demon.co.uk/masonic/report.html (Accessed October 28, 2009).

8. Bill Rankin, *Atlanta Journal Constitution*, "Tech student's terror tie revealed; Made Casing Videos," January 14, 2008, http://www.mail-archive.com/osint@yahoogroups.com/msg52871.html (accessed November 13, 2009).

CHAPTER 2: MASONIC RITUALS

1. Edinburg Register House Manuscript, 1696.

2. Chetwood Crawley Manuscript, c. 1700.

3. Quoted in R. J. Meekren's "The Symbolism of the Old Catechisms," *The Builder Magazine* 2, no. 1 (February 1926). Reprinted in Michael Poll, ed., *The Freemason's Key: A Study of Masonic Symbolism*, (New Orleans: Cornerstone Book Publishers, 2008).

4. For an exhaustive examination of this topic, see Robert L. D. Cooper's *The Rosslyn Hoax*.

5. Brown, *The Lost Symbol*, 4.

6. Brown, *The Lost Symbol*, 5.

7. Hillel Italie, "Freemasons await Dan Brown novel 'The Lost Symbol,'" Associated Press, September 15, 2009, http://www.miamiherald.com/entertainment/arts/books/story/1240148.html (accessed November 3, 2003).

CHAPTER 3: ART, CODES, AND *THE LOST SYMBOL* COVER

1. Brown, *The Lost Symbol*, 408.

2. Albert G. Mackey, *Encyclopedia of Freemasonry* (Chicago: The Masonic History Co., 1946), 296–298.

3. William Alfred Bryan, *George Washington in American Literature 1775–1865* (Westport, CT: Greenwood Press, 1979), 84.

4. Elonka Dunin, *The Mammoth Book of Secret Codes and Cryptograms* (New York: Carroll & Graf, 2006).

5. The CIA's official Kryptos web page is https://www.cia.gov/about-cia/virtual-tour/kryptos.

6. Kim Zetter, "Typo Confounds Kryptos Sleuths," *WIRED* magazine, April 20, 2006, http://www.wired.com/science/discoveries/news/2006/04/70701?currentPage=2 (accessed May 2, 2006).

CHAPTER 4: SYMBOLISM

1. The line originated with Hamlet's soliloquy, Act III, Scene 1: "*Who would these fardels bear/To grunt and sweat under a weary life,/But that the dread of something after death,/The undiscover'd country from whose bourn/No traveller returns, puzzles the will/And makes us rather bear those ills we have/Than fly to others that we know not of?*"

2. G. J. Monson-Fitzjohn, *Drinking Vessels of Bygone Days* (London: H. Jenkins Ltd., 1927), 77.

3. Brown, *The Lost Symbol*, 69.

4. Hall is frequently cited as one of the world's foremost experts on Freemasonry, at least by non-Masons and anti-Masons. He is not as well regarded in the Masonic community. His book, *The Lost Keys of Freemasonry*, was written in 1923, when Hall was twenty-two years old. He was not a Mason, and he used many discredited (and many more uncited) research books, producing a thought-provoking but historically inaccurate work that makes dubious assertions. Hall actually became a Freemason in 1954 at Jewel Lodge No. 374 in San Francisco, and interestingly, never wrote another word about the fraternity after joining. For more on Hall, see the excellent biography, *Master of the Mysteries* (2008) by *Los Angeles Times* reporter Louis Sahagun.

5. Johan Isaac Hollandus, *Die Hand der Philosophen/ mit ihren verborgenen Zeichen. Wie auch desselben Opus Saturni etc.*, (Frankfurt/M.: Th. M. Götze, 1667. Translated by Leone Muller (Restorers of Alchemical Manuscripts Society, 1986), http://www.rexresearch.com/hollhand/hollhand.htm (accessed September 17, 2009).

6. Ibid.

7. Ibid.

8. Manly Palmer Hall, *The Secret Teachings of All Ages* (Los Angeles: Philosophical Research Society, 1928), facsimile edition, 1988, LXXII.

9. Malcolm C. Duncan, *Duncan's Masonic Ritual and Monitor*, (Philadelphia: Washington Publishing Company, 1866), 53.

10. Ibid.

11. Indopedia, the Indological Knowledgebase, "Brianism," http://www.indopedia.org/Brianism.html (accessed October 15, 2009).

12. Plato's *Timaeus*, from *The Dialogues of Plato*, translated by Benjamin Jowett (1892; reprinted Charleston, SC: Forgotten Books, 2008).

13. A briefer description also appears in 2 Chronicles 3:16-17; in that version, Jachin is spelled Jakin.

14. Robert Hieronimus, *America's Secret Destiny* (Rochester, VT: Destiny Books, 1989), 48.

15. For more about the fascinating life of Cagliostro, see Philippa Faulks and Robert L. D. Cooper, *The Masonic Magician: The Life and Death of Count Cagliostro and His Egyptian Rite* (London: Watkins, 2008).

CHAPTER 5: THE SCOTTISH RITE

1. S. Brent Morris, "Misrepresentations of Freemasonry," *A Page About Freemasonry*, http://web.mit.edu/dryfoo/Masonry/Essays/b_morris-reply.html (accessed October 10, 2009).

2. Changes in the degrees of the Northern Masonic Jurisdiction occur frequently. For an exhaustive study of the history of the individual degrees in the NMJ, see *The Degree Rituals of the Supreme Council, 33°, AASR for the Northern Masonic Jurisdiction, United States of America,* by C. DeForrest Trexler, 33°. (Supreme Council, 33°, AASR, NMJ, 2008), http://supreme council.org/getfile.tpl?orig_filename=eDegreeRituals.pdf&source=dynamic/d ownloads_73.dat&ng_down_id=73 (accessed August 10, 2009).

3. Arturo de Hoyos, *Scottish Rite Ritual Monitor & Guide* (Washington, DC: Supreme Council, 33°, Southern Jurisdiction, 2008), 23–25.

4. Nesta Webster, *Secret Societies and Subversive Movements* (1924; reprint Escondido, CA: Christian Book Club of America, 2000), 139.

5. For more detail about the building of the House of the Temple, see William L. Fox, *Lodge of the Double-Headed Eagle: Two Centuries of Scottish Rite Freemasonry in America's Southern Jurisdiction,* (Fayetteville, AR: University of Arkansas Press, 1997).

6. There is no shortage of other non-Masonic buildings based on this same design. Some of them include: Grant's Tomb in New York City; the spire of St. George's Church, Bloomsbury, in London; the Indiana War Memorial in Indianapolis, Indiana; and the Shrine of Remembrance in Melbourne, Australia.

7. Margaret Hair, "Masonic house of the temple a not-so-secret marvel," *Mercury News,* July 24, 2006, http://www.rickross.com/reference/ freemasonry/freemasonry8.html (accessed November 13, 2009).

CHAPTER 6: THE CAPITOL BUILDING

1. *Columbian Mirror and Alexandria Gazette,* September 25, 1793.

2. R.W.G.M.—P.T. stands for "Right Worshipful Grand Master, *pro tempore.*"

3. *Columbian Mirror,* op. cit.

4. Psalm 133:2–3.

5. A detailed and exhaustive report of the life and work of Brumidi, as well as detailed photographs of his work in the Capitol building, including the *Apotheosis of Washington,* may be found online, published by the U.S. Congress in 1998. See Barbara Wolanin, *Constantino Brumidi, Artist of the Capitol* (Washington, DC: 103d Congress, 2d Session, Senate Document 103–27), http://www.gpo.gov/congress/senate/brumidi/ (accessed September 18, 2009).

6. Mason Locke Weems, *A History of the Life and Death, Virtues and Exploits of General George Washington.* 1809.

7. Christopher Hodapp, *Freemasons for Dummies Blog,* "R:.W:. Kwame Acquaah Elected Grand Master for GL of DC," November 6, 2008, http://freemasonsfordummies.blogspot.com/2008/11/rw-kwame-acquaah-elected-grand-master.html (accessed November 6, 2008).

8. Paul M. Bessel, "Masonic Recognition Issues," http://bessel.org/masrec/ phachart.htm (accessed October 1, 2009).

CHAPTER 7: THE WASHINGTON MONUMENT

1. Portions of this chapter have appeared previously in *Solomon's Builders: Freemasons, Founding Fathers and the Secrets of Washington, D.C.* (Berkeley, CA: Ulysses Press, 2007) by Christopher L. Hodapp.

2. The history of the Washington Monument is told in great detail in *A History of the Washington Monument 1844–1968* by George J. Olszewski (Washington, DC: Office of History and Historic Architecture, U.S. Department of the Interior, National Park Service, 1971).

3. U.S. Congress, *The Debates and Proceedings in the Congress of the United States with an Appendix containing Important State Papers and Public Document, and all the Laws of a Public Nature; with a copious Index* (1789; reprinted Washington, DC: Gales & Seaton, 1851), 804.

4. Polk was a Freemason. He was a member of Columbia Lodge No. 31 in Columbia, Tennessee. *See* William R. Denslow and Harry S Truman, *10,000 Famous Freemasons* (Missouri Lodge of Research and William R. Denslow, 1957; reprinted New Orleans, LA: Cornerstone Book Publishers, 2007), 353.

5. National Parks Service, *List of Memorial Stones with Inscriptions,* (Washington D.C.: National Parks Service, 2005) http://www.nps.gov/archive/wamo/history/appd.htm (accessed November 13, 2009).

6. *A History of the Washington Monument, 1844–1968* by George J. Olszewski. (Washington D.C.: National Parks Service, 1971).

7. Snopes.com, "*Laus Deo,*" http://www.snopes.com/politics/religion/lausdeo.asp (accessed October 20, 2009).

CHAPTER 8: MYTHS, LEGENDS, AND DAN BROWN'S WASHINGTON

1. David Ovason, *The Secret Architecture of Our Nation's Capital* (New York, HarperCollins, 2000), 459, note 59.

2. Ibid.

3. Ibid., 355.

4. H. S. Wycoff, "The Great American Seal," *The Mystic Light, the Rosicrucian Magazine,* 56–62.

5. Jean K. Rosales and Michael R. Jobe, "Who Is That Man, Anyway?" http://www.kittytours.org/thatman2/search.asp?subject=135 (accessed October 17, 2009).

6. The beautifully illustrated book, *On These Walls*, written by John Y. Cole and photographed by Carol M. Highsmith, was published by the Library of

Congress and Scala Publishers in 2008; it provides hundreds of photos of the artwork in the building, much of it in places not seen by the public.

CHAPTER 9: NOETICS

1. Barbara Bradley Hagarty, National Public Radio: "Woman Reads Dan Brown Novel, Discovers Herself," October 12, 2009, http://www.npr.org/templates/story/story.php?storyId=113676181 (accessed October 15, 2009).

2. *In the Shadow of the Moon*. DVD, directed by David Sington, 2007, Velocity/Thinkfilm.

3. Brown, *The Lost Symbol*, 502.

4. Lynne McTaggart, *The Intention Experiment* (New York: Free Press, 2007), xxii.

5. Ibid., xxiii.

6. Jonathan Leake, *The Sunday Times,* "A particle God doesn't want us to discover." October 18, 2009, http://www.timesonline.co.uk/tol/news/science/biology_evolution/article6879293.ece (accessed October 9, 2009).

CHAPTER 10: WHENCE COME YOU, AND WHITHER ARE YOU TRAVELING?

1. Brown, *The Lost Symbol*, 30.

2. *Ibid.*, 410.

3. Ralph Lester, *Look to the East* (New York: Dick & Fitzgerald Pub. Corp., 1876), 150.

4. *Albert Pike's Lecture on Masonic Symbolism and A Second Lecture on Symbolism: The Ómkara and Other Ineffable Words.* Transcribed and Annotated by Rex R. Hutchens. Washington D.C.: The Scottish Rite Research Society, 2006.

5. H. L. Haywood, "A Bird's Eye View of Masonic History," *The Builder Magazine* 8, no. 10 (October 1922).

Selected Bibliography

VObOL>OƆ ᒧᒥᒪᒣᒥᒣᒧᒧ⊏

Allsopp, Fred W. *Albert Pike, A Biography*. Little Rock, AR: Parke-Harper Company, 1928.

Anderson, James. *The Constitutions of the Free-Masons: Containing the History, Charges, Regulations, &c. of that Most Ancient and Right Worshipful Fraternity: for Use of the Lodges*. London: William Hunter, 1723.

Andrews, Francis B. *The Mediaeval Builder and His Methods*. Mineola, NY: Dover, 1999.

Baigent, Michael and Leigh, Richard. *The Temple and the Lodge*. New York: Arcade Publishing, 1989.

Biedermann, Hans. James Hulbert, trans. *Dictionary of Symbolism: Cultural Icons and the Meanings Behind Them*. New York: Facts On File, 1992.

Blanchard, Johnathan. *Scotch Rite Masonry Illustrated, In Two Parts*. Chicago: Ezra A. Cook, 1887.

Bryan, Wilhelmus Bogart. *A History of the National Capital from its Foundation Through the Adoption of the Organic Act*, Vol. I. New York: Macmillan, 1914.

Brown, Dan. *The Lost Symbol*. New York: Doubleday, 2009.

Brown, Glenn. *History of the United States Capitol*. New York, Da Capo Press, 1970.

Brown, Robert Hewitt. *Stellar Theology and Masonic Astronomy*. New York: D. Appleton & Co., 1882.

Carrington, Henry Beebee. *The Obelisk and its Voices; or the inner facings of the Washington Monument with their lessons*. Boston, Lee and Shepard: New York, C.T. Dillingham, 1887.

Chevalier, Jean and Alain Gheerbrant. John Buchanan-Brown, trans. *Dictionary of Symbols*. London: Penguin, 1996.

Clark, I. Edward. *The Royal Secret*. Louisville, KY: J. P. Morton & Co., 1923.

Coil, Henry W., ed. *Coil's Masonic Encyclopedia*. 1961. Reprint, Richmond, VA: Macoy Publishing Company, 1996.

Cole, John Y. and Highsmith, Carol. *On These Walls*. London: Scala Publishers, 2008.

Conner, Patrick, ed. *The Inspiration of Egypt: Its Influence on British Artists, Travellers and Designers 1700-1900*. Brighton, England: Croydon Printing Company, 1983.

De Hoyos, Arturo. *Scottish Rite Ritual Monitor & Guide*. Washington, D.C.: Supreme Council, 33°, Southern Jurisdiction, 2007.

Denslow, William R. and Harry S Truman. *10,000 Famous Freemasons*. Missouri Lodge of Research and William R. Denslow, 1957. Reprint, New Orleans, LA: Cornerstone Book Publishers, 2007.

Duncan, Malcolm C. *Duncan's Masonic Ritual and Monitor*. Philadelphia: Washington Publishing Company, 1866. Reprint, New York: Crown Publishers, 1986.

Dunin, Elonka. *The Mammoth Book of Secret Codes and Cryptograms*. New York: Carroll & Graf, 2006.

Farrah, George. *The Temples at Jerusalem and Their Masonic Connections*. Hinckley, Leicestershire, England: Central Regalia Ltd., 2003.

Faulks, Philippa, and Cooper, Robert L. D. *The Masonic Magician; The Life and Death of Count Cagliostro and His Egyptian Rite*. London: Watkins, 2008.

Ford, Kenneth W. *The Quantum World, Quantum Physics for Everyone*. Cambridge, MA: Harvard University Press, 2005.

Fox, William L. *Lodge of the Double-Headed Eagle: Two Centuries of Scottish Rite Freemasonry in America's Southern Jurisdiction*. Fayetteville, AR: University of Arkansas Press, 1997.

Fox, William L., ed. *Valley of the Craftsmen: A Pictorial History Scottish Rite Freemasonry in America's Southern Jurisdiction, 1801-2001*. Washington, D.C.: Supreme Council, 33°, Ancient and Accepted Scottish Rite of Freemasonry, Southern Jurisdiction, U.S.A., 2001.

Hall, Manly Palmer. *The Secret Teachings of All Ages*. Los Angeles, CA: Philosophical Research Society, 1928. Facsimile edition, 1988.

Harper, Kenton N. *History of the Grand Lodge and of Freemasonry in the District of Columbia*. Washington, D.C.: R. Beresford, 1911.

Hieronimus, Robert. *America's Secret Destiny*. Rochester, VT: Destiny Books, 1989.

Hodapp, Christopher L. *Freemasons For Dummies*. New York: Wiley, 2005.

Hodapp, Christopher L. *Solomon's Builders: Freemasons, Founding Fathers and the Secrets of Washington, D.C.* Berkeley, CA: Ulysses Press, 2007.

Holmes, David L. *Faiths of the Founding Fathers*. New York: Oxford University Press, 2006.

Hutchens, Rex R. *A Bridge to Light: The Revised Standard Pike Ritual: A Study in Masonic Ritual and Philosophy*, 3rd ed. Washington, D.C.: The Supreme Council, 33°, Southern Jurisdiction, 2006.

Jacob, Margaret. *Living the Enlightenment*. New York: Oxford University Press, 1991.

Jacob, Margaret. *The Origins of Freemasonry*. Philadelphia, PA: University of Pennsylvania Press, 2006.

Knoop, Douglas, and G. P. Jones. *The Mediaeval Mason*. Manchester: Manchester University Press, 1967.

Lester, Ralph P. *Look to the East*. New York: Dick & Fitzgerald Pub. Corp., 1876.

Lévi, Eliphas. A. E. Waite, trans. *Transcendental Magic*. London: Rider & Co., 1896.

Longstreth, Richard, ed. *The Mall in Washington, 1791-1991.* Washington, D.C.: National Gallery of Art, 1991.

MacNulty, W. Kirk. *Freemasonry: A Journey through Ritual & Symbol.* London: Thames and Hudson, 1991.

Matthews, Jean V. *Toward a New Society: American Thought and Culture 1800–1830.* Boston: Twayne, 1991.

McClenachan, Charles T. *The Book of the Ancient and Accepted Scottish Rite of Freemasonry: Containing instructions in all the degrees from the third to the thirty-third, and last degree of the rite, together with ceremonies of inauguration.* New York: Press of A. H. Kellogg, 1901.

McTaggart, Lynne. *The Field: The Quest for the Secret Force of the Universe.* New York: HarperCollins, 2002.

McTaggart, Lynne. *The Intention Experiment.* New York: Free Press, 2007.

Meyer, Jeffrey E. *Myths in Stone: Religious Dimensions of Washington, D.C.* Berkeley, CA: University of California Press, 2001.

Mitnick, Barbara J., ed. *George Washington: American Symbol.* Manchester, VT: Hudson Hills Press, 1999.

Monson-Fitzjohn, G. J. *Drinking Vessels of Bygone Days.* London: H. Jenkins Ltd., 1927.

Morris, S. Brent and John W. Boettjer. *Cornerstones of Freedom: A Masonic Tradition.* Washington, D.C.: The Supreme Council, 1993.

Newbury, George A. and Louis L. Williams. *A History of the Supreme Council, 33° of the Ancient Accepted Scottish Rite of Freemasonry for the Northern Masonic Jurisdiction of the USA.* Lexington, MA: Supreme Council AASR, NMJ, 1987.

Ovason, David. *The Secret Architecture of Our Nation's Capital* (originally published as *The Secret Zodiacs of Washington, D.C., Was the City of Stars Planned by Masons?*). London: Random House UK, 1999.

Page, Thomas Nelson. *Washington and Its Romance.* New York: Doubleday, Page & Co., 1923.

Pike, Albert, and Rex R. Hutchens. *Albert Pike's Lecture on Masonic Symbolism and a Second Lecture on Symbolism: The Ömkara and Other Ineffable Words.* Washington, D.C.: Scottish Rite Research Society, 2006.

Pike, Albert and Arturo De Hoyos. *Albert Pike's Esoterika: Symbolism of the Blue Degrees of Freemasonry.* Washington, D.C.: Scottish Rite Research Society, 2005.

Poll, Michael R., ed. *The Freemasons Key.* New Orleans, LA: Cornerstone Book Publishers, 2008.

Poll, Michael R., ed. *Masonic Enlightenment.* New Orleans, LA: Cornerstone Book Publishers, 2006.

Price, David Hotchkiss. *Albrecht Dürer's Renaissance: Humanism, Reformation, and the Art of Faith.* Ann Arbor, MI: University of Michigan Press, 2003.

Ridley, Jasper. *The Freemasons.* New York: Arcade Publishing, 2001.

Roberts, J. M. *The Mythology of the Secret Societies.* London: Watkins Publishing, 2008.

Robinson, John J. *Born in Blood: The Lost Secrets of Freemasonry.* New York: M. Evans & Company, 1990.

Scott, Gary T. "Masonic Stones of the Washington Monument," *Heredom: Transactions of the Scottish Rite Research Society,* 5 (1996): 253.

Shaw, George Bernard. *Annajanska, the Bolshevik Empress.* Studio City, CA: Players Press, 2002.

Stevenson, David. *The Origins of Freemasonry: Scotland's Century 1590–1710.* Cambridge, MA: Cambridge University Press, 1988.

Tabbert, Mark A. *American Freemasons: Three Centuries of Building Communities.* New York: New York University Press, 2005.

Tatsch, J. Hugo. *Freemasonry in the Thirteen Colonies.* New York: Macoy Publishing & Masonic Supply Company, Inc., 1933.

Tresidder, Jack, ed. *The Complete Dictionary of Symbols in Myth, Art and Literature.* London: Duncan Baird Publishers, 2004.

Unwin, George. *Guilds and Companies of London*. London: Methuen & Co., 1908.

U.S. Congress, *The Debates and Proceedings in the Congress of the United States with an Appendix containing Important State Papers and Public Document, and all the Laws of a Public Nature; with a copious Index*. Washington, D.C.: Gales & Seaton, 1851.

Uzzel, Robert L. *Eliphas Lévi and the Kabbalah*. Lafayette, LA: Cornerstone Book Publishers, 2006.

Webb, Thomas Smith. *The Freemasons' Monitor; or Illustrations of Freemasonry*. Salem, MA: Cushing & Appleton, 1818.

Weeks, Christopher. *AIA Guide to the Architecture of Washington, D.C.*, 3rd ed. Baltimore, MD: Johns Hopkins University Press, 1994.

Weems, Mason Locke. *A History of the Life and Death, Virtues and Exploits of General George Washington*, 1809.

Artwork Credits

Artwork Credits

Index

┌▣⊐◻≫

Index

Other Ulysses Press Books

SOLOMON'S BUILDERS: FREEMASONS, FOUNDING FATHERS
AND THE SECRETS OF WASHINGTON, D.C.
Christopher Hodapp, $14.95
Solomon's Builders guides readers on a Freemason's tour of Washington, D.C., as it separates fact from myth and reveals the background of the sequel to *The Da Vinci Code*.

ATHEIST UNIVERSE: THE THINKING PERSON'S ANSWER TO
CHRISTIAN FUNDAMENTALISM
David Mills, Foreword by Dorion Sagan, $14.95
Clear, concise and persuasive, *Atheist Universe* details exactly why God is unnecessary to explain the universe and life's diversity, organization and beauty.

COMPLETE KRAV MAGA: THE ULTIMATE GUIDE TO OVER 230
SELF-DEFENSE AND COMBATIVE TECHNIQUES
Darren Levine & John Whitman, $21.95
Developed for the Israel military forces, Krav Maga has gained an international reputation as an easy-to-learn yet highly effective art of self-defense. Clearly written and extensively illustrated, *Complete Krav Maga* details every aspect of the system, including hand-to-hand combat moves and weapons defense techniques.

COURAGE AFTER FIRE: COPING STRATEGIES FOR TROOPS
RETURNING FROM IRAQ AND AFGHANISTAN AND THEIR
FAMILIES
Keith Armstrong, LCSW, Paula Domenici, PhD
& Suzanne Best, PhD, $14.95
Foreword by Senator Bob Dole
Deals with the repercussions of combat duty, including posttraumatic stress symptoms, and outlines specific ways to reintegrate into families, workplaces and communities.

THE DEAD SEA SCROLLS REDISCOVERED: AN UPDATED LOOK AT ONE OF ARCHEOLOGY'S GREATEST MYSTERIES
Stephen Hodge, $13.95

While providing a comprehensive introduction to the Dead Sea Scrolls, this book also takes a fresh look at many controversial questions: Why were the scrolls written? Are they prophetic? How are they related to Christianity and Judaism?

GODLESS: HOW AN EVANGELICAL PREACHER BECAME ONE OF AMERICA'S LEADING ATHEISTS
Dan Barker, Foreword by Richard Dawkins, $14.95

In *Godless*, Barker describes the intellectual and psychological path he followed in moving from fundamentalism to freethought.

LONDON'S WAR: A TRAVELER'S GUIDE TO WORLD WAR II
Sayre Van Young, $16.95

A unique guide to the history and still-visible reminders of London's heroic resistance, *London's War* is the first guidebook to explore the sights and attractions related to World War II and London's Home Front.

THE SIX UNSOLVED CIPHERS: INSIDE THE MYSTERIOUS CODES THAT HAVE CONFOUNDED THE WORLD'S GREATEST CRYPTOGRAPHERS
Richard Belfield, $14.95

Brings to life the amazing stories and fascinating structures of the secret codes that have stubbornly resisted the efforts of the world's best code-breakers and most powerful decryption software.

To order these books call 800-377-2542 or 510-601-8301, fax 510-601-8307, e-mail ulysses@ulyssespress.com, or write to Ulysses Press, P.O. Box 3440, Berkeley, CA 94703. All retail orders are shipped free of charge. California residents must include sales tax. Allow two to three weeks for delivery.

About the Author

JUE<> >ПО J<>ПЕF

Christopher L. Hodapp is the editor of the *Journal of the Masonic Society*, and the author of the bestselling book, *Freemasons For Dummies*. He has been a Freemason since 1998, and is a Past Master of two Masonic lodges.

His second book, *Solomon's Builders: Freemasons, Founding Fathers and the Secrets of Washington, D.C.*, was published by Ulysses Press in 2006. He has also co-written *The Templar Code For Dummies* and *Conspiracy Theories & Secret Societies For Dummies* with his wife, Alice Von Kannon.

Hodapp has spent more than twenty-five years as a commercial filmmaker. In 2009, he was featured in *Secrets of the Founding Fathers* for the History Channel, and *Hunting The Lost Symbol* for the Discovery Channel. He lives in Indianapolis.